Also by William Woodruff

Paradise Galore

Billy Boy: The Story of a Lancashire Weaver's Son

*Impact of Western Man: A Study of Europe's Role in
the World Economy, 1750–1960*

*America's Impact on the World: A Study of the Role of
the United States in the World Economy, 1750–1970*

The Struggle for World Power, 1500–1980

The Emergence of an International Economy, 1700–1914

A Concise History of the Modern World: 1500 to the Present

Vessel of Sadness

Vessel of Sadness

William Woodruff

Foreword by Martin Blumenson

BRASSEY'S

WASHINGTON • LONDON

First Brassey's edition 1996

Library of Congress Cataloging-in-Publication Data
Woodruff, William.
Vessel of Sadness/William Woodruff; foreword by
Martin Blumenson.—1st Brassey's ed.
p. cm.
ISBN 1-57488-054-3
1. World War, 1939–1945—Italy—Anzio—Fiction.
2. Anzio Beachhead, 1944—Fiction.
I. Title.
[PR6073.062V4 1996]
823'.914—dc20   95-37253

Designed by Tanya Pérez

10 9 8 7 6 5 4 3 2 1
Printed in the United States of America

To those who died on the plain of Latium,
January 22–May 26, 1944

Foreword

A FRIEND HAS GONE.
HE HAS DRUNK HIS VESSEL OF SADNESS.
HIS BATTLE IS STILLED.

After being privately published in the United States, William Woodruff's *Vessel of Sadness* appeared in England in 1970 to acclamation. British reviewers were unusually moved and touched by what they described as the book's "desolating realism" of "war's total madness." With good reason, they called the book "brilliantly written," containing a "thread of poetic vision" and a "hectic immediacy" that captured "with almost unbearable fidelity the atmosphere" of war, "the unvarnished but rivetting truth," "the authentic, gut-twisting fear of the soldier in battle."

Placing Woodruff alongside Hugo, Stendhal, Hardy, Remarque, even Homer, the reviewers linked his account of combat directly to those of the fine British writers who had described the terrors of trench warfare in the Great War of 1914–18. The connection is apt, for Woodruff was British—

born in Lancashire in 1916; serving in the 1st British Infantry Division in World War II, he landed with his unit in the initial wave of the Anzio invasion and fought in the subsequent battle on the Anzio beachhead, a static action at viciously close range that was reminiscent of the First World War's Western Front.

Perhaps these reasons explain the essential difference between Woodruff's narrative and several splendid American works that detail personal experiences during the Second World War. Charles B. MacDonald's classic *Company Commander*, the story of an infantry leader in Europe; Donald Burgett's *Currahee!*, an account of paratroopers in the Normandy invasion; Janice Holt Giles's *The Damned Engineers*, a selection from her husband's letters from Europe; and sailor Patrick Fahey's *Pacific Diary* are examples. While instructive and interesting, none of these carries the emotional impact or the exquisite literary quality of Woodruff's account.

War is hell, Sherman said, but according to Woodruff almost a hundred years later, it is death. The killing and the dying, often random and senseless, occur at the end of a long line that starts with the rationales of policy and runs through the bureaucracies of mobilization, strategy, logistics, doctrine, tactics, and leadership to the bloody and brutal battlefield, where the individual fighting men confronting the enemy are the cutting edge of the immense organization of warfare. The people on the line of contact are the agents of the impersonal combat power of the nation.

Thus it was at Anzio, conceived and approved in the highest councils of state, planned at the top levels of command

and staff, ordered by army, corps, division, regiment, battalion, company, platoon, and squad, and carried out by the
soldiers who unprotestingly obeyed the orders and did the
fighting.

The Anzio landings were a gamble designed to capture
Rome quickly. Having invaded southern Italy in September
1943, the Allied armies of Great Britain and the United
States were weary by the end of the year. They had battered
their way up steep mountains and across swift rivers,
through narrow corridors and over coastal plains. Everywhere they were under the eyes and the guns of the Germans, who skillfully used the natural advantages of the
terrain for their defense. Giving way grudgingly in the face
of superior Allied firepower, the Germans reduced Allied
progress to a turtle's pace. They stopped the Allies before
Cassino, well below Rome, the only significant milepost in
the campaign. Unless the Allies could break open the dog-
ged defenders with a spectacular move, they were doomed
to follow what seemed like an endless road to the capital
city.

When the Western Allied leaders, Franklin D. Roosevelt
and Winston S. Churchill, met with Josef Stalin in Tehran
at the close of 1943, they decided to launch from England
the cross-Channel attack, Operation Overlord, in the
spring. Because the Normandy invasion appeared to be a
desperate venture, Roosevelt and especially Churchill
wished to inflict a strong psychological blow on the enemy
beforehand. Rome, which the Germans held tenaciously,
seemed more than appropriate for the purpose. If Rome fell
to Allied arms before other Allied troops crossed the Chan-

nel, the invasion of France would have a better chance of success.

This they told Generals Sir Harold Alexander and Mark W. Clark, who led the Allied forces in Italy. The few remaining months before Overlord gave the theater commanders little time to reach Rome. Because the agonizing push up the Italian boot offered little prospect of getting them there by spring, they decided to go by water. By making an end run and going around the difficult ground, by sending troops and weapons, equipment and supplies to Anzio by ship, they would bypass the German defenses, come in behind them, dislodge the Germans from Cassino, and prompt them to withdraw to Rome and beyond. The technical risks were enormous, but they had to be accepted if the Allies were to meet the deadline.

Although the sea voyage to Anzio and the debarkations were relatively easy, Field Marshal Albert Kesselring, who headed the German forces in Italy, refused to panic. Holding his troops firmly at Cassino on the main front, he collected a massive contingent of forces and contained the Allies in a small and crowded beachhead around Anzio. From the Alban Hills overlooking the harbor, German guns pounded the Allied units. From airfields near Rome, German planes strafed and bombed Allied installations. And between the Mediterranean and the mountain, on the ancient Pontine Marshes drained and reclaimed by Mussolini's modern government, men met and killed and died. From January 22, 1944, when the Allies came ashore at Anzio, until May 25, when the forces on the main front linked up with the beachhead, Allied and German soldiers fought at close quarter.

Rome is about an hour's drive from Anzio, but in 1944 it took the Allies more than four months to get there. Across that landscape torn by shell and bomb and bullet, the soldiers left a trail of blood and anguish. The beachhead was ten to twelve miles wide, seven or eight miles at its deepest, constricted and dangerous no matter where. Exposure, exhaustion, trench foot from freezing days and nights in foxholes half filled with slush and water, as well as the lethal weapons of man, produced close to seventy-five thousand killed, wounded, missing, injured, crippled, and hurt Allied and German soldiers and innocent Italian civilians.

These are the bare facts of the situation in which Woodruff's tale unfolds. He gives no more than an intimation of the mechanics of war, for he is uninterested in the military machinery. He is absorbed by the bloody hell of the battlefield, an insane world, and by the behavior of men caught up in an incomprehensible and insufferable event.

We have always tried to disguise or obscure or overlook what happens on the field of battle, for it is cruel and inhuman. We talk of personnel or troops or units or forces instead of men. We speak of destroying the enemy or his will to fight, of seizing ground or a hill, of penetrating the enemy line, of maneuvering and outflanking, bombing and shelling and firing, of inflicting casualties, of attacking and defending. But what it all comes down to in the final analysis is killing human beings. Whatever the ideological issues or political questions, whether they be simply the survival of a nation or a society or a group, what activates a soldier in contact with the enemy is the need to kill those who would kill him. This single-minded lust underlies warfare, and Woodruff exposes it not as stemming from superhuman drive but rather as flowing out of profound fear and rage.

"Never think that war," Ernest Hemingway once said, "no matter how necessary, nor how justified, is not a crime. Ask the infantry and ask the dead." And yet, as Sidney Hook has written, "The arm is no more powerful than the will behind it, and no wiser than the ideas that guide it." The problem, as Woodruff makes clear, is that men in the midst of irrational carnage have neither the time nor the inclination to perceive or to ponder the facts, the virtues or truths, the ideals or way of life that ultimately motivate war. The firing line, which may be nothing more than a hole in the earth, has temporarily eliminated them. But they exist beyond or behind the terror, as Woodruff suggests, and ultimately they sustain men and make most of them overcome the brutality.

Except for the particulars of time and place and weapons, combat is very much the same as it has been from Thucydides and Xenophon to Vietnam. If the primary impulse on the battlefield is self-preservation, it frequently takes second place, paradoxically, to courage and self-sacrifice. For Woodruff is hardly celebrating battle or death. He has written an accusation against the futility of war, a warning against the degraded and ignoble, and, more especially, a testament to hope. "After four years of war," he says, "the magic has gone out of most things in life. Nobility remains." And if that disappears from our world, God forbid, despair will be all.

William Woodruff, graduate research professor in economic history at the University of Florida, is a living exam-
ple of the strength of the human spirit, of how men scarred
by an inferno of death can be healed to well-being. Dedi-
cated to scholarship and learning, Professor Woodruff
graces his campus, and wherever he goes, with his civilized
and cultured sensitivity.

In his book the main character is war. His victims are the
fighting men who hate not the enemy, but war itself. His
thrust is the struggle for life in the midst of devastation. His
logic is not of right or wrong but of dead or alive. His prose
depicts the position of man in industrialized warfare and
focuses not on individual heroes but rather on mass heroism. His moral is the continued existence, in the midst of
confusion and heartbreak, of nobility, the nobility of self-
sacrifice for others.

Why did he write the book? He answers, "To tell of war
through the fragmented impressions in the minds of men."
In his quest to present those highly charged emotions, he
sought "the universal, the intimate, and the timeless." He
tried to "paint a picture of men I knew" within the frame-
work of "the plight of humanity." All who fought on both
sides of the front "were locked in the same human di-
lemma." His story is literature, and history, too, "if history
is concerned to reveal how people felt and thought and lived
and died in the past—in human terms." For, says Woodruff,
"The purpose of art, or of literature, or of history is identical: to seek the essence of the human condition."

This is truly his subject, and he has handled his investiga-
tion with great insight and skill. Deceptively simple in lan-

guage and imagery, frightening and upsetting, frank and un-flinching in view, *Vessel of Sadness* helps us understand the nature of man in a world where there is as yet no alternative to the desolations of war.

—Martin Blumenson

These things I saw,
and a great part of them I was.
—Virgil

Vessel of Sadness

Prologue

It was late afternoon before he reached the little fishing port by the Tyrrhenian Sea. The golden light of the setting sun had begun to turn to gray. The Alban Hills had drawn around them their nightly scarf of mist. On the highest peak a great fire glowed. A white bull had been slain. Caesar himself had witnessed the sacrifice. Jupiter was appeased. All men could now walk together in peace.

The traveler caught sight of the water before he caught sight of the town. Antium lay hidden behind a fold of the Latium plain. But he knew where the road would suddenly dip down to the sea. It was here that he had learned of the goddess Fortuna and it was here that over the years he had continued to make his pilgrimage. He jogged along the seafront for a little way, the donkey's hooves echoing on the paved road, the gulls swooping down and screaming above his head. Then he turned into a narrow courtyard. As he *dismounted, he praised the gods for bringing him safely once more to Antium.*

Going to the shrine of Fortuna the next morning, he was shocked to hear from a man that Caesar had been assassinated. For a few moments he looked down helplessly at the glass vessel containing his tiny offerings, which had slipped from his grasp and now lay shattered at his feet. Then he entered the grove of the goddess Fortuna in whose hands all knowledge of the future lay.

1

A candle flickered in the corner of a stable on an Italian hillside, casting its moving shadows against the wall and among the darkened rafters. The cattle stalls were empty. A group of British soldiers were sitting on a pile of straw playing cards. Cigarette smoke rose above them. Someone was playing carols on a mouth organ. Outside was a snow-covered world and a starlit night. Great pointed icicles hung from the barn roof ready to fall into the yard below with the crash of glass. Except for a stray shell exploding in the distance, all was quiet. Soldiers kept watch. Above them was the abbey of Monte Cassino, the oldest monastery in Christendom. It was Christmas Eve, 1943.

A sergeant entered the stable and talked with a corporal lying on a straw-filled manger. The corporal muttered, rolled out of the manger, swore, and went into the adjoining room. The carol playing ceased, the laughter stopped.

"The patrol's on," he said matter-of-factly. "I'll need two of you."

"Hasn't Sarge heard it's bloody Christmas Eve?"

"The war hasn't. The war's greedy."

A bunch of matchsticks protruded from the top of the corporal's clenched fist.

"Shortest two goes."

"Depart 2200 hours, check and briefing at 2100 hours. Nothing new about it: out by way of the bridge, along the river, up the creek, through the wood, around the bottom of 'Polski's Hill,' up and over Hangman's Hill, across the open ground to 'Lofty's Farm' (they say the wolves took Lofty's body out and messed it about), then across the open ground to the woods, praying nobody's watching, then into cover, across the road at 'Burned-out Corner' and home again. Just about the time that we go out," he added, tucking his stocking cap into the back of his tunic, "the Yanks will attack Hill 730. I'm not going to dispute my share of 730. It's a graveyard up there."

"Rome by Christmas!" murmured the man shuffling the cards. "The general must have been mad. It isn't reasonable to have so many mountains! I wonder if the travel posters are still on the wall outside Charing Cross station. 'Come to Sunny Italy!' "

The corporal wriggled down into the straw again and continued to stare into the rafters. He didn't care about the war anymore. He had almost reached the desperate stage when he wouldn't care about surviving. He had fought his way across North Africa. Then he had fought his way up here from Salerno. Through orange and lemon groves, through great stands of evergreens, somber pines, and great oaks. Then into the craggy mountains, through defile after defile, sometimes with the help of a mule, sometimes along mountain tracks where a mule couldn't go and the soldiers were the beasts of burden. Always onward it seemed, through fog and rain with little to eat and that stone cold. He'd been in the fight for the bridge at Scafati, where Richard had copped it. That's when something inside him had broken. A crowd of them had then crossed to the coast and struggled across the blue shoulder of Vesuvius. At an observatory tower on the western slope of the mountain they had rested with their backs against chestnut saplings and had looked upon the immensity of sky and sea and mountain, disbelievingly.

There had been no rest when they got into Naples; they had rushed after Jerry to the Volturno. In pouring rain they had struggled to cross the river at Capua, only to be driven back. The Yanks got across higher up. After that it was one hill after another—through little whitewashed villages clinging to the mountainside like swallows' nests—until they'd reached the banks of the Garigliano. Outside one little place with a saint's name, they'd been met by a little group of black-dressed women, their hands pressed together in prayer, who had beseeched them to go away, that their village might be spared. It hadn't been spared. It was a queer little place, nailed at a drunken angle to the side of a ravine. It did what they had expected it to do. When Jerry put a barrage of heavy mortars down on its head, the village gave up the ghost and slid into the ravine, children, grandmothers, and all. They had cast the little bunches of mountain flowers that the women had given them after the train of ruin down the mountainside, sadly.

The laughter broke out again next door. The man with the mouth organ was having difficulty with "Good King Wenceslas." Somebody kicked on the door and bawled out "Christmas Eve booze is up." There was a scramble for mess tins, weapons, and helmets.

A *Feldwebel* carrying a submachine gun ran down the steps of a deep underground shelter in the vicinity of Monte Cassino. He drew back a heavy curtain concealing the entrance to a crowded, smoke-filled, ill-lit dugout.

"Achtung! Tonight's patrol will consist of the following. . . ." He read nine names.

"Jawohl!"

Some of the acknowledgments could hardly be heard.

In less than two minutes he had dropped the curtain back into position and was out in the snow-covered street. For a moment he looked up at the abbey and the star-filled sky. He sniffed the cold air and listened. Somewhere in the vicinity of a bombed church he heard the singing of "Stille Nacht."

"Here, mate, watch the wire. 'Peace on Earth' is the password, and for Christ's sake come back quietly. Good luck, chum."

A British sentry standing by a snow-covered stone wall watched the patrol as it crossed the field and was swallowed up into the night. The sentry stamped his feet. Somebody had said this was the worst Italian winter in living memory.

Nine men moved on in the darkness, silently, isolated, a little ship in a hostile sea. They passed through a gate thrown back across a dirt road, filed past a row of flattened mud huts that led to abandoned vegetable allotments. They then reached an open meadow. The first nervousness was passing. The hard tightness in the chest had eased off and the trickle of sweat down the spine had ceased. With luck, it would be no worse than the loss of another night's sleep.

The path dipped down toward the river. Normally there was a good deal of loose gravel here, which made an awful noise under heavy boots—even when you wore socks over them to muffle the noise. Now the blanket of snow quieted the earth. The only sound was the crunch of snow as the men followed each other down the slight incline toward the water. It was quite dark and slightly warmer. The patrol shifted course to the right when the first clump of willows came into sight. Something squawked at the side of the water. There was a *plop* as an animal left the ice and entered the river.

The corporal had covered this ground a dozen times in the past two months. Usually he had followed the platoon sergeant, but tonight he was out on his own, in front. With the river on his left he felt happier about his bearings. One day from a forward post he had watched a heron standing in the shallows about here. Not long ago, curlews and peewits had risen from this meadow when a shell exploded. Two days ago, he had studied the bank of the river for hours through his glasses without seeing a bird of any kind.

The corporal slowed down until he was sure that all his men were with him. Without speaking he made off upstream. The others followed. Over on the right in the direction of Hill 730, a considerable battle was developing. The hills were silhouetted against the sky as the light cast by the shell explosions blinked on and off. A red flare rose and fell, giving the hillside a fiery glow. A great chandelier of light fell into the battle area turning night into day. The blinding light was reflected from the dark clouds above the mountains. That nasty woodpecker noise coming from the mountainside was German heavy machine guns. Quite deadly; one peck and men went down like lumps of wood, arms and legs sticking out in all directions. It made you afraid of all machines. The light machine gun that Number 8 carried, at the end of the section, was a peashooter compared to the "heavy."

There was a slight movement ahead and the corporal tensed himself and peered into the darkness. Something scurried across the snow. The patrol continued.

At the opening of a creek running inland across the meadow into the foothills the nine men halted to rearrange their loads. For a few minutes they crouched on their haunches and listened. Except for the fighting on Hill 730 and some sporadic shelling across the river there was no noise. The men spoke in the slightest whisper, faces close together. They took a short swig from the corporal's flask as a small plane hovered above their heads. Who knew, the plane might go slamming into the hillside. Anything, as long as it didn't drop a flare followed by a canister of bombs.

Number 2 didn't care whether the plane was friend or foe.

His face and hands were getting numb with cold. He cursed the snow, he cursed the war, and he cursed the winter, especially this winter filled with rain and cold and mud and snow and death. Monte Camino had been his first real taste of fighting mud, rain, and Germans. For ten days on the slopes of Camino, he and his comrades had fought all three, and had been defeated by all three. Exhausted to the point of weeping, they'd been dragged out of the line and plopped down in a wet meadow within sound of the guns. They'd been ordered to rest. Monte Camino was still there when they went back into action. It still blocked their path. It had rained so heavily that the general had called the next offensive Operation Raincoat. The rain wasn't deceived, nor the mud, nor the Germans. His mob had almost perished on a hilltop called La Bandita. They'd fought all day to see whose hill it was. Then torrential rains had washed out the battle. He had spent the night standing huddled against another fellow in a hollow tree. The rains had stopped the next morning, but by then they were like drowned rats and it was all they could do to bring in the wounded and bury the dead. It was from there, in November, that they got their first real look at "Monastery Hill." They had been looking at it and fighting for it ever since. Monte Cassino was a door sealing the entrance to the Liri Valley, the Alban Hills, and the approaches to Rome. The Germans intended to keep it shut.

The patrol turned up the creek into the hills. Several

more low-flying planes flew over in the direction of Hill 730. Explosions followed as the planes dropped antipersonnel bombs. In the dark it was like trucks tipping out loads of heavy stones. By the time the anti-aircraft guns had got into action the sound of the light planes had almost died away.

At the end of the section, Number 8 was dragging one of the legs of the machine-gun tripod through the snow, causing a snakelike furrow to follow him in the dark. Number 8 was listening to the explosions in the distance. He kept well up against Number 7. Where he could, he stepped into Number 7's footprints in the snow. It was easier that way. He watched the bowed head in front of him. He wondered what was going on in Number 7's head. But what did it matter what was going on in other people's heads? He followed his instincts. They'd got themselves into this pickle by people thinking too much. People who just sat and thought and thought were like birds who sat and preened and preened and who never used their feathers, or laid an egg. Number 8's ambition was to keep a full belly, stay safe, get home, and at all costs avoid the thinkers. What price thinking when it landed you on a perishing hillside, on a Christmas Eve, far from home with the fear of death inside you?

For some time now the patrol had trudged along—nine men lost in their own little world. They had followed the creek until it ran into the wood. They had avoided the intersections and had crossed the lanes among the trees quickly. From the edge of the wood they had climbed "Polski's Hill." For a week or two this hill had been inhabited by an unhinged Polish soldier who, from a lair, rained death on anybody who passed by. Polski had foxed both sides. He should not have been there, and the clown did not distinguish between friend or foe. In time, he had run out of ammunition and had marched back to his battalion across a minefield in the pitch dark singing his head off. The Poles had packed him off somewhere without a scratch on him. "Doing a Polski" was a phrase already being used by the soldiers for anybody who managed to avoid the reaper by acting daft.

After "Polski's Hill" they climbed up Hangman's Hill. The going was tougher up the hillside and they halted now and again to get their breath. It was when they got up there that the snowstorm began. It began slowly. No more than the odd flake striking the eye. Later, a cascade of starshells falling upon Monte Cassino revealed the abbey silhouetted against a snow-filled sky.

Number 7 was oblivious to the snowstorm. His mind was fixed on a pathetic little airmail letter in his pocket. It was from his wife telling him that she had been unfaithful and was about to bear a child. It had been snowing gently when he'd gotten the letter earlier in the day. He'd stood in the farmyard with the other fellows around the post corporal laughing and joking. When he had read the first few lines he had found it difficult to understand what his wife was trying to say, and he had started at the beginning again. Slowly the truth had borne in upon him. There was to be a child, of his wife, her first child, but not of him.

For a little while he'd leaned against the barn wall holding the letter before him, reading it, rereading it. The snow-flakes had thawed on the notepaper, causing the ink to run. But the ink had run in parts of the letter where the snow had

never fallen. They were his wife's tears. Later he had
thought he was going to go mad if he didn't tell somebody
what had happened, so he had told his mate. His mate had
looked at him for a long time queerly and then had said,
"Look, Bernie, your missus isn't the only one in England
with a bun in the oven."

It was three A.M. on Christmas Day. There was still heavy
fighting on Hill 730. A blizzard was blowing. It had snowed
heavily since midnight. The snow now came in great blinding gusts. The patrol had halted close to "Lofty's Farm."
They were huddled together in the lee of a wall. The corporal was peering in the direction of the farm, brushing the
snow out of his eyes. He was worried. Should he get into
"Lofty's Farm" and stay there until darkness returned
again? Or should he dig in here against the wall? Or should
he make a run home on a compass bearing? All they had to
do was to keep their backs to the din coming from Hill 730
and follow their noses. They would be sure to strike the
river. He knew how to cut corners in this country. The more
the corporal thought, the more confident he became that he
could get his team home, even allowing for the blizzard and
the depth of the snow. Battalion knew of his predicament
and would help him with radio. Only trouble with the emergency system was that Jerry knew all about it, too. Jerry
sometimes tagged on and came home with you, knocking
you off just when you got cocky and careless and were about
to duck through your own wire. It was dangerous. But then,
sitting out here was dangerous too. And it was Christmas
Day.

There was more quiet talking among the group sheltering

in the lee of the wall. Suddenly the corporal got up from where he was crouched.

"All right," he said quietly, "let's go home then. We'll have to bunch up and we'll have to move."

There was a last little drop of rum in his flask. He drank it. Then he left the protection of the wall and the others filed after him. The snow-filled wind now broke over the patrol like a giant wave. It hurled itself upon them, driving a great white spray through their open legs as they marched. It tugged at their clothing, buffeted them, raced and swirled around them like a spinning top, blinding them.

The German saw the British corporal first. He fired, taking off the top of the corporal's head. Two seconds later both leaders were lying in the snow, dying. Terror seized both sides: there were shots, shouts. Six or seven bodies fell almost at once. A few Germans plowed their way back to the shelter of the wood and four of the British scrambled through the snow toward the wall they had just left, the fear of death upon them. The snow soon lay trampled and bloodstained. Deep footprints radiated across the hillside. Patches of snow were already dyed deep red. A trail of blood ran to the edge of the wood. One man almost gained the shelter of the trees, only to topple over into the deep snow. He raised himself up and then fell back again, as if the effort was not worthwhile.

Somewhere in the wood a wounded man was calling, a howling wind drowning his cries. A single shot rang through the hills across the snow. Abandoned equipment lay everywhere. The snow continued to fall in great puffs. The branches of the evergreens sank closer to the earth.

The dawn of Christmas Day, 1943. The blizzard had passed. The rising sun caused the cedars to cast their long shadows before them. On Hangman's Hill a rabbit was scratching at the deep snow trying to reach the soil below. A glistening white blanket covered the earth. Only the red holly berries stood in contrast to the whiteness of the snow. From the wood the calls of a wounded man were heard, weakly and infrequently. In the Christian world they were celebrating the birth of Christ. On the skyline, in the candlelit, refugee-crowded chapel of the monastery of Monte Cassino, an old priest wearing his vestments ascended the altar, arms outstretched, to say the first Christ Mass.

2

A British Army jeep wound slowly up the steep road that led from Carthage to the village of Beni Abbās on the Tunisian coast. As the jeep whined and groaned its way upward the morning mists slipped away. A dark imposing structure emerged out of the clouds in front of the vehicle and joined itself to the earth. This was the Villa Beni Abbās, earthbound, yet soaring above the Mediterranean with a view of the sea, the land, and the sky of startling beauty. The jeep passed through a beflagged entrance and came to a halt before British sentries in a great cobbled courtyard. A junior officer got out. He was the first to arrive at an Allied conference called to decide upon an amphibious landing to seize the city of Rome. It was Christmas Day, 1943.

* * *

The billiard ball ran swiftly down the green-carpeted table, glanced off another ball, and deposited itself in one of the pockets. With the conference only an hour away a group of staff officers were finishing their game. An army servant entered with a tray of drinks. Another soldier brought a clean leather belt, which he helped his officer to put on. Bets were being taken for and against a seaborne landing at Anzio in Italy.

The odds were just being read out by an officer who had been scribbling on a piece of paper.

"For: Break the deadlock at Cassino. Cut the lifeline of the Tenth German Army in the South. Capture Rome with tremendous effect on Allied and German morale. Give the Russians less to complain about. Set the right precedent for D-Day in the West. Anzio can be got at with limited shipping facilities, it offers open country for quick movement to the hills, its flanks are protected by rivers and marshes, it is close to Allied airfields, and the massed artillery of men-of-war is available offshore.

"Against: An invasion force of 150,000 men can't hope to throw the Germans off balance. Intelligence shows the presence of a formidable striking force of armor in the area. The beachhead is dominated by the enemy on the Alban Hills. Winter storms could isolate the invading force. The beaches are unsuitable. There is insufficient shipping to maintain the beachhead. Troops experienced in amphibious landings are not available. An unsuccessful landing at Anzio might cause a setback to the entire Allied strategy for the invasion of western Europe."

"Whatever the odds," a senior officer said quietly, "this is probably the last time in this war that we in Italy shall occupy the center of the world military stage."

A servant appeared at the door.

"The general's coming up the hill, sir."

"Very well," said the officer, concentrating on his shot. Having made a successful stroke he replaced his cue in the rack and left the room with several other officers. For them the conference had begun.

*

A crowded conference room,
A cloud of tobacco smoke,
Ashtrays filled with cigarette and cigar butts.
Eager faces, tired faces, sick faces, fit faces.
The constant rustle of paper.
Big men sitting in their appointed places
Saying nothing, knowing all.
Lesser men who do the work, minds honed to a razor's edge.
Lesser men with souls, lesser men without,
Behind whom sit their servers as at High Mass.

Men who have misgivings:
"Must we bleed on two fronts instead of one?"
Mad men who know only their star,
From whom for man's sake the bit must be hidden.
Men who pity men. Men who know only machines:
"Now if four hundred two-and-a-half-ton
  trucks loaded to a capacity
  of five tons are required

to land a minimum maintenance
supply on D plus one,
  how many trucks will be required if . . . "
Men who sit apart with expressionless eyes,
Mummies, friendless, still.
Many-headed men, whispering together, deciding play.
Men of world stature with intoxicating tongues.
Men who come and go with wood and water.
Is this the innocence of guilt, the jigsaw of justice?

*

The wintry sun had fallen quickly into the Mediterranean Sea; darkness had come to the Carthage peninsula. The Villa Beni Abbās had returned to the sky. Great clouds of mist had rolled inland from the bay, causing the outside of the villa to run with sweat and the cobbles in the courtyard to glisten with dampness under the headlamps of the passing vehicles.

"Heh! Do you know where Anzio is?"

"No, why?"

"Well, they've decided to storm the beaches there in a month's time. Be good to get past Cassino."

"Where is Anzio?"

*

Tiled roofs, moonlit.
Quiet streets,
Fishing vessels riding at anchor.
A little town by the Tyrrhenian Sea,
Asleep,

Unaware,
Unsuspecting.

*

The first day of January 1944. A room at the palace of Caserta, Army Group Headquarters, Italy. Landscaped gardens, fountains, terraces, and tree-lined drives. In one of the rooms in the palace a general was about to address a group of officers.

"Gentlemen," he commenced, "a happy new year to you all. You are well aware that a decision was made recently at Tunis to carry out a landing in strength in the Anzio-Nettuno area. The code name given to that landing is 'Shingle.' You know with what object: to outflank the main German army holding the southern front anchored upon Cassino and to seize Rome. You know that D-Day is the twenty-second of January, that is, in three weeks' time, and that the first troops will go ashore at oh-two-hundred hours. The decision to make the landing is settled, so is the time of landing. There will be no discussion here today on these points. This morning I shall deal with some of the problems that have arisen concerning *how* we shall carry out the invasion."

At that point the general was interrupted by a bewhiskered colonel sitting in front of him.

"More important, sir," he said, "I wish you'd say a little more about *who* shall carry out the invasion."

"Ah, yes," said the general with an enigmatic smile, "I shall come to *who.*"

* * *

The camp commandant at No. 17 Transit Camp, Bizerte, on the North African coast, prepared to pick up his hat and cane from the table where he had placed them while addressing the survivors of the troopship *Carmania*, sunk in the Mediterranean a week ago.

"I realize, gentlemen," he said as he prepared to leave the room, "that for me to tell you a week ago that you would return to the United Kingdom on survivors' leave and now for me to tell you that you are going to be sent to Italy as reinforcements is not a very pleasant thing to do, and I can appreciate what a bitter disappointment you have experienced. I can only say that, like you, I obey orders. Orders change according to the situation, and while I do not pretend to know what is happening or going to happen in Italy, it is fairly clear that an emergency has arisen there. I am sure that if Army Headquarters could have avoided this change of orders they would have done so. In any event you are already aware that survivors' leave according to army regulations is a privilege, not a right. I am instructed to tell you that this change is already in process of being conveyed to your next of kin in Britain. That is all," said the camp commandant, as he moved toward the door. "Thank you for your attention."

The poker school was curled up on a great coil of rope in the transit camp at Algiers. Archie was resourceful. He'd just come in from the darkness with a great sanitary pail full of steaming coffee.

"You're a gent, Archie," his pals said as they quickly

dipped their tin mugs into the hot brew and drank his health. Despite the windfall of the coffee it was obvious that the school was uneasy. They had talked themselves hoarse about the things they'd do when they got home, and here they were about to embark for Italy.

They'd been snatched, that's what they'd been. And they didn't like it.

"A stinking way to start a new year," Archie said. He didn't know where Italy was, he didn't care where Italy was, he never wanted to see Italy.

"Not on your bleeding life," he had told the sergeant who had snatched him. "I'm going home." He had even pushed his way in to see the camp commandant. He was telling the poker school about it.

"Well, I stands in front of 'im and I says, 'My old pappie is expecting me. This might kill 'im,' I says."

"You old fixer," said one of the school, digging Archie in the ribs.

"No, honor bright," said Archie, "it's against my principles to get snatched like this. My folks would never forgive me."

"And what did 'Camp' say, Archie?" asked one of the school.

"Well, truth is," said Archie, dealing a fresh hand, "I came away feeling sorry for Camp. Camp's tired and he rambles. He talked about spiders' webs."

"Spiders' webs!" said a short little fellow who had just started the betting.

"Spiders' webs," said Archie, as though he and Camp shared a profound secret.

" 'I see your point of view, soldier,' Camp said to me,"
Archie went on, between bids, " 'and I'd like to help you.
But my job is body snatching and you've got to go.' It was
then Camp talked about spiders," said Archie.

" 'Look, soldier,' Camp said, 'what happens to you in this
war is not my decision, it's not yours, it's the spider's. You've
got yourself entangled in the web. Now stop struggling.
Take comfort, soldier, the spider might never get to you.' "

" 'Struth," said one of the players sweeping up the kitty.
"Camp's gone round the bend. Happens to everybody after
three years abroad. We'd better get back home fast. We
could get hurt."

"Well," said Archie, "I too felt sorry for Camp, but when
I came out of 'is office I remembered my old pappie's advice:
'Damn the field marshal's baton, son. Just keep the army's
worries off your back!' Camp's worries weren't my worries.
Besides I'd no intention of any spider eating me, so I decided
to give the Doc a go."

"It's malingerers like you, Archie," said an enormously
fat, contented-looking member of the school, "who gets sick
people like us into serious trouble."

"Oh, I don't know," said Archie, "I felt bad enough. The
thought of crossing the Med again fair gave me cramp and
nausea."

"Bet there'd have been no cramp and nausea," said another, winking at Archie, "if the old ship had pointed its
nose towards the Thames."

"Well, anyway," said Archie, continuing, "I felt it was
worth a go, so I went to see Doc. After Doc had tried to push
my foot over my head and failing that down my throat, 'e

said, 'Soldier, in my opinion you're suffering from one of two things, you're either pregnant or you've got battle nerves. As you haven't seen a battle or heard a shot fired in anger, I can only assume you're pregnant.' And there was I without sufficient strength to pick up my pants!'"

The poker school broke into uproarious laughter. They dug Archie in the ribs again. They laughed until some of them cried. Play was held up. Archie laughed as much as the others. He'd read somewhere in a book that "he who worries, dies twice." Dying once, which Archie regarded as the ultimate in bad luck, was too much for him. He'd have nothing to do with anything that meant he'd have to die twice.

"Don't volunteer for anything," his pappie had warned him when the military had eventually grabbed him. "Stay in the center of the rear rank with your mouth shut, don't go anywhere unless you've got to." But hadn't his pappie also said: "If you've got to go, son, make the damned best of it!" Well, so Camp's blasted spider had got him. He'd tried to get out of the web and couldn't. Damn Camp, he was going to go on trying; meanwhile, he was going to make the best of it.

"Your turn to deal, Shortie," he said, passing the cards. Then he dipped his mug into the sanitary pail for a second time round.

The telegraph boy stood his bike against the wall and brought the knocker of number 76 down again with a hard clang. He was only a youth, but this delivering of wartime telegrams had got on his nerves. Only yesterday, it seemed, most telegrams were messages of joy—a birth, a remembrance, a win on the football pools, somebody coming home. Poor as these people were in the dreary North of England cotton towns, they would always dash back into the house and find a threepenny bit for his troubles or, failing that, a piece of cake. Give them a telegram now and they would burst into tears and gently close the door in his face. Nobody likes to go round giving bad news all the time. He stood in front of the little door with its paint peeling off, holding the sealed message in his hand.

Except for the number on the door there was nothing to distinguish this house from the hundreds of other little houses that stretched into the distance on both sides of the street. It was a gray street with its wet slate roofs capping the "two up and two down" houses that stood side by side, back to back in an unbroken line for miles, until they almost reached the factory gates where the occupants spent most of their working lives. Suddenly, there was a movement behind the door at number 76. The youth prepared himself to get rid of the War Office telegram as quickly as he could and get away. Instead of signing for it, the woman who came to the door tore open the envelope. He watched her face. He knew at once he'd delivered a winner. She told him her bloke was coming home on survivors' leave and gave him sixpence. As she closed the door he could hear her calling out excitedly to her children, "Dad's coming home, Dad's coming home."

To help himself stay awake Major Watkins began to tap his polished field boots with his swagger cane. But for the sheer discomfort of his chair he would have fallen asleep long ago. After three hours of conference at Caserta Palace, nothing new had emerged about the Anzio invasion. If someone had taken a duster and erased all the technical data that had been chalked onto the blackboard the whole thing might be forgotten. It was men who would make the difference on D-Day. Nobody talked about men. What would these officers be able to tell their men when they went back? Nothing, except that the job still had to be done.

He stifled still another yawn and wondered what Charles III of Spain, whose palace this had been, would have thought of it all. After a morning like this he certainly would have needed a drink.

3

A young soldier was lying on the crowded floor of an ill-lit brush factory near Naples. Because of rats his kit was hanging from the rafters above his head. Two days ago at the rehearsal on the beaches south of Salerno he had almost drowned. But for Nobby he would have drowned. In the dark, the big ships had opened their mouths and pushed out the little ships, many of which became swamped and sank in the rough sea. He'd never seen so many landing craft sink. They said forty craft had been lost just at the rehearsal. The way the big 105-mm guns had stuck their great noses into the air as the vessels sank had fascinated him. His squad had been lucky; they'd survived. Even if they did reach the wrong beach at the wrong time. But Sarge had wept. "Do this on D-Day," he'd warned, "and you'll be as cold as mutton." The boy soldier began to mumble in his sleep.

"TNT to blow the rear door of the pillbox? Check. Phosphorus grenades to lob through the blown door? Check. Fuses? Check. Check. Check. The yellow lamp, ours is the yellow lamp. Go for the yellow lamp. Red on the left, green on the right. Watch the current. Don't slip. If you slip you're a goner. Grab the guide rope. Follow Nobby. Keep close to Nobby. Hang on to Nobby, Nobby knows."

The boy's calls began to wake other soldiers, but they left him alone. Instead, some of them lit cigarettes and blew the smoke into the rafters.

Why, there is Father Kelly with his embarkation bib on again instead of his full vestments. That settles it, we're off.

"In the name of the Father and of the Son and of the Holy Ghost, amen."

The server doesn't have any vestments on at all. Just watch the server's empty bayonet scabbard getting in his way as he bobs up and down at the altar. Fancy an altar on an empty ammunition box! But it's all the same to Father Kelly: packing cases, a fallen tree trunk, a grand piano, a kitchen table. Remember the time we moved into the sand dunes on the North African coast, forming up ready to follow the tanks in a full-scale attack? It was too beautiful a day to die. All was fresh and clean. Great puffs of cloud, blue sky, and a great sea pounding away on the beach. A little farther inland the cannons were trying to destroy each other. And in the middle of all this, while we were praying that Jerry wouldn't spot us forming up, Father Kelly had appeared and celebrated Mass on a heap of sand, the soldiers flopping down on their knees around him. Then they got up and followed the tanks with their colored pennants fluttering proudly in the breeze as they went into battle.

What enormous hobnailed boots the server has! Wonder if everybody's boots look as big as that? Look out, here comes the Elevation.

"This is my body, this is my blood."

Wonder if Father Kelly realizes what a crummy mob he's saying Mass to? Can't go to Communion. Didn't go to confession. Ought to have gone to confession last night when we'd the chance. It's six A.M. here. Wonder what time it is at home? If we get the chopper the Lord had better see us as we are. Anyway, good old Father Kelly is coming with us and he's a glutton for confessions under duress. At Salerno he took confessions in his stride, running with the boys up the beach. If we get the chopper the odds are Father Kelly will be there to help us over.

Double rations for breakfast. No queuing. Grub sticks in your throat a bit. It isn't that the blokes serving the grub want you to get knocked off, but the only reason you're getting double rations is that you might get knocked off. Eat the grub anyway; stuff it down. What you can't stuff down stuff in your pockets. If this show goes like the others, you're going to need it. Now get your kit on. Help each other. Pack your lucky charms (of course, no one believes in lucky charms but we take them just the same), give away your loot. There goes the sergeant major bawling out his lungs. He gets his face so red we call him "Furnace." The way he shouts "Everybody outside," you'd think he didn't want us to miss the show. Well, let's go. The markers are out. The pipes are present, so are the drums. "Eat-em-up-Joe," the colonel, is out there. Never seen him look so smart, or so lean, or so gray, or so spoiling for a fight. Good old "Eat-em-up-Joe" took no notice of his Yank boss when he said that the battalion should move to the ship quietly.

"Begging your pardon, sir," "Eat-em-up-Joe" is said to have replied, "for three hundred years now my people have gone into battle with the sound of the pipes and the drums ringing in their ears. They wouldn't know how to fight any other way."

That is how he led us to the banks of the Clyde four years ago. Watch out, old "Furnace" is bawling the order: "Battalion—fall in!"

We're off, and the pipes give you a bonnie feeling.

Naples docks. An armada is forming. Formalities the same as last time: "Fill in this card. Here's a pencil. You can't die without filling in a form. Here's your last air letter. Use it well, laddie. Hand it in tonight, if there is a tonight."

Here we go. Up goes the gate. Sheep driven on. Gate drops. There's Vesuvius, also Capri. Lots of heavy shipping out in the bay. A big show this, whatever it is.

The landing craft is pulling away.

"Good luck, fellows. God speed!"

"Aye, we'll be thanking you kindly now, but you can be keeping the speed to yourself."

The quayside recedes. The bay echoes to the call of every

kind of vessel. Shrill tones, low, low bass. The pipers and drummers are marching to and fro on the jetty. The skirl of the pipes remains with us until we are well out.

The convoy sailed at dawn the next day, the twenty-first of January, in a calm sea, at five knots.

4

It was night. An Allied battle fleet was crossing the Tyrrhenian Sea heading in the direction of Anzio. A heavy sea was breaking over the bows of the leading cruiser. On the bridge the captain was giving instructions into an instrument. The ship's enormous guns were slowly raised and stood against the darkened sky. Automatically, great shells were brought from the bowels of the ship. Slowly, the breech of one of the great guns swung open. A white-smocked attendant pressed a button and the shell trundled inside the giant maw of the gun. The breech gate swung to.

A cat furtively crossed the Via Aprilia, leading to the main promenade of Anzio, leapt a wall, and disappeared. A shutter of a neighboring house flapped to and fro in the wind. Sud-

33

denly, feet were running down the street. They turned into the vestry house by the church. A hand reached for the knocker and began to beat the door, the noise echoing from the surrounding houses. The priest's head appeared at an upstairs window. There was excited calling. Bernadini's child was dying. Would the priest bring the holy oils? The feet raced out of the vestry gate. The shutter continued to flap to and fro in the wind.

In the Villa Angelina a phone rang. A bedside light was switched on. A gray-haired Italian diplomat had been expecting the call. He knew how the Gestapo worked. They had arrested Alverado earlier in the evening in Anzio. It would not have surprised him if instead of calling from Rome thirty-five miles away the Gestapo had walked unannounced into his bedroom.

On the line was his office in Rome. An emergency had arisen. Would he please return to his office at first light? He agreed. He knew that a Gestapo man would be waiting for him. Even the Roman physician who had innocently allowed him to use the villa for a few days would have difficulty clearing himself. By the time the Gestapo had finished with this house many of the priceless art objects would have disappeared for good. Antiques, books, paintings, furniture, tapestries—they'd take the lot. A pity that his personal drama should bring suffering to this quiet corner of Italy, where life was still rustic and peaceful. The land was still cultivated; only that morning he had seen a mother laboring in the fields with her three boy sons and a tired ox. The great well-kept orchard surrounding the villa was dormant now but in the spring it would be rich with blossom and, later, fruit. He set the alarm for four A.M., made an entry in his diary, and turned out the light.

A peasant's little mud-colored farmhouse. A German soldier's uniform thrown over a chair. The German was sleeping with the peasant's daughter. This was the best kind of war. He was a peasant among peasants. The sons of the family were dead. He was a German and they were Latins. But he was a man and their sons had gone. Men were scarce. He was needed for the farm and he loved the daughter. There was friction at first, especially with the family, but all that was in the past. When the war was over he would marry the girl and stay here. They needed him badly. Already he had repaired the barn and tended the neglected fruit trees. The soldier was awakened by the cold. He got up, took his greatcoat from behind the door, gently covered the girl in the bed, and joined her under the extra cover.

Private Bottomly was rereading the letter that he had written to his wife, Maude. He must have read it six times. What was there to say? A few days ago he had been told he was going home on survivors' leave. Now he was taking part in an invasion. He couldn't tell her about the landing. He told her the usual things. But at least half the air-letter form was still untouched and it stared at him accusingly. He knew full well that if he let himself go he'd fill it in no time. But what he would say might be looked upon as self-pity. After all, they weren't the only couple caught in this thing. And Maude had enough worries. So he went on about the weather, and the holidays they'd had together at the seaside before the kids were born, and the good food they were getting, and that he was doing what Maude had asked and was changing his socks and underwear regularly. Eventually, the letter was written; the unused space was filled in. A big box had been provided for mail at the end of one of the ship's gangways. He went along and threw in his letter.

Thank goodness, he thought, as he returned to where he had been sitting, one thing he didn't have to tell Maude was that he was on an ammunition ship. No sooner had the convoy got out of the Bay of Naples than the captain had told them that lifebelts need not be worn. If they were hit by enemy fire lifebelts would be of no earthly use.

Well, he was sure nobody wanted an ammunition ship to explode in their midst. The captain probably had a wife and kids, too. At least it would be quick—even odds, dead or alive. When an ammo ship exploded there were never any "in betweens."

Private Bottomly sat himself down again and fell to wondering what Maude would do if the worst happened. Perhaps she would remarry—at least for the kids' sake. He'd never thought of Maude remarrying. The idea struck him as silly. After a while, he got up and joined a crowd of fellows who had formed a ring around four soldiers. They had discarded their weapons and were dancing a reel with complete abandon, accompanied by the clapping and the calling of the other soldiers and a man who played on a long tin whistle.

5

It was one minute to H-Hour: 0150 hours, January 22. In a few seconds' time many people unconscious of the sword that hung above them would die. On the command radios men were straining their ears. Perhaps there would come a dramatic last-moment order to hold fire, as at Pantelleria a year ago? Or would it be Salerno all over again?

It was a cold, clear night, yet dark to those who had just emerged from the lighted bowels of the ships. All was quiet on land and sea. A light breeze was blowing onshore. Since just after midnight the great invasion fleet had edged its way silently toward the land and had dropped anchor three miles off Cape Anzio. Out at sea warships had taken up their stations, ready. Smaller men-of-war clung to the flanks of the convoy to ward off attack. The minesweepers had gone ahead to clear the channels through which the assault would be made. In the assembly area patrol boats moving through the darkness had herded the first waves into formation and had led them off into the night. Twenty-seven fighting battalions—fifty thousand men—were ready to storm the beaches. Aboard all ships was an intense stillness. As the second hand moved toward H-Hour even the davits used to lower the lighter vessels into the sea fell silent. All men watched and waited. The immensity of what was about to happen struck them speechless. The jokes and the conversations of a few minutes ago had tailed off and were now forgotten. All guns pointed shoreward. All decks were cleared for action. There were ten seconds left. How long, how long, Lord, can ten seconds be!

Suddenly, the shoreline rose in convulsion. Men, trees, houses, earth, stones were flung skyward. An intense rocket barrage had begun. Farther out at sea the heavy naval guns winked death upon the land. The sky was rent by an insane, howling, shrieking madness. A giant thunder filled all men with fear. The land erupted into great orange flames. Star shells, flares, shell bursts, and gun flashes fitfully banished the darkness and cast a ghastly ocher glow over land, sea, and sky. In the direction of the Alban Hills heavy bombing was taking place. All eyes turned shoreward. As the preliminary bombardment ended there was an ominous silence from the land.

A few moments ago men had spoken in tense whispers or stood silently waiting. Now the radio sets spluttered into life and voices were everywhere. Boats were being lowered away. Men, preparing to disembark, called out the names of their friends or their regiments in the dark. There was a last adieu. The naval signal lamps betrayed the presence of a vast armada. Thousands of troops were clambering into the little cockleshells that would carry them to the beaches. In a few minutes' time some of the young noisy bodies dropping into the landing craft would be rolling backward and forward in the surf, idiotically lifeless; either that, or stiffening on the beach.

The flash of guns revealed scores of little ships rolling toward a dark, silent shore. It was a relief when the enemy batteries awakened. Sporadically, enemy shells began to fall into the water—the steel sides of the larger vessels echoing to every explosion. Instinctively, the men crouched down and huddled together. A landing craft took a direct hit and disappeared in a foaming, gurgling mass into the darkness. There were no cries, no mess. From the sea a great barrage was going on. The explosions onshore were moving farther inland. Many of those clambering into the assault craft had no sense of time, or order, or being—they knew only chaos and fear.

Suddenly the rope holding landing craft number 16 was slipped and the vessel charged through the water. Once away from the protection of the mother ship there was silence in the little boat as it rolled shoreward. The waves pounded the bottom of the craft, determined to break it. Icy-cold spray drenched it. The force of shells bursting in the water struck the side of the vessel like hammer blows.

As the door fell into the water with a great splash the first squad began to disembark. There followed shouting and cursing, cries for help. The vessel was stuck on a sandbank. The soldiers looked at the black current swirling before them. Somebody tossed out a couple of lifebuoys with little red lights attached to them, but they went swirling off in the current as if they were in a millrace.

The cries of the drowning men faded away into the darkness.

A sodden little boat drifted helplessly toward the shore. It tossed about so much that some of the soldiers were sick. Suddenly, it struck the beach and the gate went down with a rattle.

The water was intensely cold. It lapped round their bellies, filled their trousers and their boots. The soldiers struggled in the dark, not knowing where they were putting their feet. Sarge was already ahead, making for a lamp flashing from the beach. A corpse was rolling and slopping about in the surf.

The man with the lamp was crouched against a wall. He was a sailor. He continued to signal as he shouted at the soldiers: "Jerry has packed up. Take the white tape. The dunes are heavily mined. Some fellows have copped it in the dunes."

At that moment an explosion at the water's edge threw the man with the lamp into relief against the stones. The flash of light revealed six or seven soldiers sitting with their backs to the wall watching him. Somebody had dragged them out of the way and propped them against the wall looking out to sea. Their heads were in the most grotesque positions.

The soldiers took the tape and began to climb upward across the dunes. Men were calling out. The water gurgled in their boots as they struggled through the deep sand. German batteries were firing overhead. Suddenly, with a *plop*, *whine*, *clap*, the men came under mortar fire. They went down into the sand instantly, sheltering their heads against each other's legs. The mortar fire stopped as abruptly as it had started. It had covered the men with wet, stinging sand.

They got up again, shook themselves, grabbed the tape, and made for the road—this time faster than before. Unidentifiable objects were smoldering and hissing with flame and smoke among the trees.

After a few minutes they broke through some scrub and followed the tape until it hit a track, which eventually came out on a long straight coastal road covered with a canopy of pines. On the road was a group of German prisoners, herded together like sheep.

The roadway was beginning to fill with Allied soldiers. Without heavy casualties they were getting into each other's way.

Sarge led his platoon across the road and up a lane in the direction of a farm—the company's first objective.

The soldiers were glad to get off the crowded road. It was dangerous, standing there waiting for the metal to come crashing down. Besides, their wet legs needed exercise, and on the road a feeling of anticlimax was quickly setting in.

As they strode along in single file across the rising ground they could sense the cold, open, dark plain in front of them. They passed a row of little cottages; at least that was what they supposed they had been before the barrage. They were all flattened and smoking now. At the side of the lane on a heap of rubble, in the dark, with a little boy on her knee, was an old woman. They were sobbing and weeping. They must have been frozen stiff out there in the cold. They gathered from her that the *tedeschi* had gone up the lane followed by the *inglesi*. Someone offered the boy a piece of chocolate, but the child wouldn't take it. They left the old woman clutching the chocolate and crying.

The platoon reached the farm before those already there had had time to move on to the next objective. Things were going much faster and easier than anybody had predicted.

As they entered the farm they passed a British light-armored tracked vehicle, which had been hit right on the nose as it plowed up the lane through the mud. The driver had been flattened against the side. The half-track had caught fire and there was an awful smell of gunpowder and burning flesh. The man's comrades had evidently tried to pull the poor devil out but must have given up in disgust. What was left hung over the side.

In the farm several squads were mixed up. There was some confusion. Sarge told the platoon to shut mouths and dig. They obeyed, digging into the soft wet soil. Only after their eyes had become accustomed to the dark did they see the body of a dead German lying right alongside them. They might have stuck their trenching tools into him. He lay facedown in a patch of beets and was quite cold.

Just when the platoon had finished digging their holes

they were ordered to take a villa on the other side of the Anzio–Albano road. Off they trooped through the wet fields. They could see nothing except the fireworks going on. There was a good deal of fighting farther inland where the brigade that had made the initial assault had got itself tangled up with the retreating German defense battalions. There were scattered fires across the countryside. A big barn was roaring away nearby, lighting up the fields for miles, it seemed, and casting great shadows. When its roof suddenly caved in, a cloud of sparks went shooting into the sky. Every building, every haystack, every copse had its perils. And running into other friendly patrols in the dark didn't help. Down on the beach a ship had been hit, lighting the sky. Planes buzzed about. The anti-aircraft fire was more dangerous to the soldiers than to the airmen. Every now and again great chunks of metal from the exploded shells came whizzing down and buried themselves in the soft earth.

The patrol crossed the wet, squelching fields of stubble, with patches of thin crackling ice, until it came to the main axis of advance, the Anzio–Albano road. There they learned that the German defenses had collapsed. Anzio and Nettuno had been captured and the sunken ships used by the Germans to block the harbor were already being hauled away. There wasn't going to be a fight for the port of Anzio. The Germans weren't showing their usual toughness. At this rate they'd be in Rome in no time at all.

The patrol crossed the road and went along the front of a wood where a British battery of twenty-five-pounders was barking away at the enemy.

They turned inland with the sea at their backs. They went

up a dark track parallel to the main road. The German gunners were beginning to wake up on the Alban Hills. Their gun flashes made the patrol uneasy as it tramped along.

It was still dark when the soldiers came to the back of the Villa Angelina, some distance from the sea. The place was shuttered and locked. It was quite a mansion, set in trees among orchards. There were several outhouses and a well standing in the middle of a yard. A dog was barking furiously. Sarge made his dispositions in case the house was full of obstinate Germans spoiling for a fight. After a few minutes a door opened and there was the sound of women shrieking. Several of the patrol went in and made a search. Some began to dig in around the house, away from the trees. Others began to make a strong point close to a large haystack.

Inside the villa candles were burning and the windows were heavily curtained. The hysterical women looked at the soldiers as if they'd fallen from the sky. There weren't any Germans there, they said. Why didn't the soldiers go away? Look at the mess their boots were making on the carpets! Sarge told the women that the troops were going to blow out the candles and then knock out the window frames and doors. The idea was too preposterous for the women to grasp, and it was only when Sarge began to tear down the drapes and knock out the windows that the idea penetrated their heads. Screaming and pandemonium followed. So Sarge shut all the women up in a back room with candles and let them shriek at each other there. The army needed the place. Although well concealed by trees, the Villa Angelina looked straight at the Alban Hills.

Sarge said it was the villa's fault for standing at a strategic point on the plain. In any event the owner was a half-wit for leaving the stuff here. Most of the world was at war. Before all the curtains were dragged down, one of the fellows took a candle to look at the paintings. He said they were worth a fortune. Not to the soldiers they weren't. They'd have swapped the lot for a hot meal. Then they put out the lights, completed the job of tearing down the curtains, and began to knock the upstairs window frames into the front garden. The windows made an awful din as they went crashing down. More troops had arrived and were helping to carry bags of earth upstairs. Others were active across the road, in the plain. A couple of officers arrived with a radio set and began to make an observation post upstairs. Some of the troops were uneasy about the big sets. They believed that Jerry could home in on them—either from the air or by shellfire. In the dark, the heavier furniture and the big beds were heaved through the holes where the windows had been. Then the walls were reinforced and the window frames blocked in with sandbags. A good number of the heavier volumes from the library were used for additional protection. The mattresses and the bedding were set down against a wall in the hope that some soldiers might get a sleep there later on. They moved about in the house and grounds in the dark, not sure whether the shadowy figures passing them were friend or foe.

*   *   *

A great white parachute flare floated slowly downward. Beneath it, standing stark against the night-clad earth, was the town of Frascati in the Alban Hills. It was early in the morning of D-Day. Another flare followed, swinging gently backward and forward like a giant chandelier, then another. Soon the whole town was bathed in a phosphorescent glow. Only an experienced listener could detect the faint note of an airplane high above the Alban Hills. Few Italians were listening; they had already buried themselves beneath whatever shelter they could find. With their nightclothes wrapped around them and their infants in their arms, they crossed themselves repeatedly and waited for the bombs to fall. An earlier Allied raid had cost them more than a thousand dead. Would the Virgin Mary see that justice was done and ensure that the bombs fell on the Germans, or would the price be paid, once more, in Italian blood?

"Hail Mary, full of grace, the Lord is with thee . . . Pray for us sinners now and at the hour of our death, amen."

The Hail Marys rolled from dry mouths. Would this be the hour of their death? They would not be kept long in doubt. The engines of the fighter bombers were already thundering above the town. As the first bombs fell the wailing of the air-raid siren ceased abruptly.

Three hours had passed. It was still dark. The Italians in Frascati were still trying to recover their dead and injured. At the entrance to the Villa Aldobrandini, German soldiers were marking off the bomb craters caused by the raid. In the dark, dispatch riders were coming and going; the noise of their engines rose and fell as they picked their way around the holes in the roadway.

* * *

January 22, 0230 hours. A bunker at German Army Group Headquarters north of Rome. A sleeping figure. A knock on the door.

" 'Case Richard'! They have taken the port intact."

"Unmöglich! Incredible! With our mobile reserves of armor and infantry just cast into the furnace of the southern front! What to do?"

" 'Case Richard'! Drums have already sounded in the Rome area, on the Adriatic, in northern Italy, in the Balkans, in France, and in the homeland. By nightfall thirty thousand men will face the invader."

"It is four hours to dawn. How many hours till nightfall?"

6

Streaks of light in the eastern sky. Soldiers peering into a still-darkened plain, wondering. Soldiers strangely quiet. Cocks crowing in the yard for the last time. Guns finding their voices. A group of reconnaissance troops in the plain beyond, alone, in the shadows, frightened, using the muzzles of their guns to feel their way. An antitank crew kneeling, waiting. A battalion of infantry, dug in, ready, thin on the ground, behind them only water. In the sky friend and foe, blind. Night, departing secretly, unobserved.

Jerry didn't strike back that first dawn, and after a while we became more casual and went about our business, and brewed some tea, and ate some pack rations, and had a smoke. Then the sun began to shed its light and warmth across the cold damp plain. Gradually, it triumphed over the mist and the clouds. A faint outline of mountains appeared in the sky. They seemed to form an enormous, smooth, dark gray mass covering the horizon. There were towns on the slopes. Their tightly packed houses gave the appearance of having slipped off the mountainside and spilled onto the plain, twisting and turning like a river that had broken its banks. They were light-colored and contrasted sharply with the darkness of the plain and the hills. Somebody said Albano was on the left and Velletri on the right. The hills wore a great white scarf of mist. The plain itself was dotted with two-story mud-colored farmhouses.

At noon two sections were ordered to put in a flank attack against a group of Germans in a farm. The weather was fine, there was no wind, the visibility was excellent.

They set out, sixteen of them, clinging to two jeeps. They were in good spirits as they bounced in and out of the shell holes. Without their weapons they might have been a group of lads off to meet the girls at a picnic.

Suddenly they came under shellfire. The road in front of them became great smoking craters. Sarge gave the order to take cover and they threw themselves against the wet earth. The jeeps stood empty, forlorn, under the trees by the road.

Sarge said they'd get on as soon as Jerry looked the other way. But Jerry didn't. He was looking right down his gun barrel at them. The fire switched from the road to the field, the shells taking great scoops of earth and flinging it into the sky. They were terrified to the point of panic as the fused shells exploded above their heads, throwing down a lethal rain. The sixteen men became a mass of humanity, clinging together, hugging the ground. Someone was hit in the leg. They could hardly go back, so it was decided to make a run for it up the road. They ran for it, their trouser and tunic buttons torn off by shell blast. They leapt on the jeeps, and bounced through the still-smoking shell holes in the direction of their comrades fighting around the farm.

It was then that it happened. In broad daylight they overshot the turning to the right, which would have taken them to the farm, and went smack into a machine-gun nest. Sarge had just said, looking around, "Here, what the—" when the gun fired the first burst. Jerry must have thought they'd gone off their heads. Two jeeploads of clinging bodies at point-blank range!

The first jeep behaved as if the steering column had broken as the vehicle pitched drunkenly toward the ditch. Then the other jeep shuddered to a halt as if struck by a hundred steel bars. Only then did they realize that the noise they had heard was a machine gun firing almost in their faces. Sarge called out, "Jump for it!" Those still able to jump for it did so. But their luck was out. The ditch was no safer than the road.

Of course, they should have hit back: "the best defense is always rapid and well-directed fire." Instead, they fled for their lives and were at the mercy of their instincts. They never even saw the enemy or his gun. Perhaps the fire came from behind the steel side of the bridge that ran across the railway in front of them; they were too terrified to find out. As they lay in the ditch they suddenly heard the fire making its way toward them. The vegetation jumped and twitched before their eyes. The bullets hissed and splashed as they struck the little pools of water close to their faces. They were sick with fear. It was as if a madman had suddenly got loose and was running up and down the ditch lashing out with chains. When the unseen chain hit a man he just crumpled up or got to his knees and moaned. Sarge shouted but every man was for himself. They were terrified of dying. When the fire lifted for a moment and went back to the road, the mad scramble began again.

It wasn't the army manual of arms that saved two out of sixteen; it was an enormous cylindrical, cement storm drain that ran underneath the road and into which two men eventually scrambled. They would have overshot the drain but for Sarge. They were too panic-stricken to see it. He himself overshot it by a couple of paces. He turned and yelled, "Into the drain!" and in one of the soldiers went with the other fellow on top of him.

Sarge only got his head and arms in. The two men pulled him in as quickly as they could, but he was quite dead. He never made a sound. So they laid him between them and his blood and later his urine went trickling down the drain. They sat opposite each other with their backs to the drain wall and their bottoms in the water, and a now sodden corpse between them. They never spoke. They just stared at each other and gasped for breath. The color had gone from their faces, and their cheeks were sucked right in, like an old man's. If someone had come down the ditch at that moment and tossed a grenade into the drain, neither of them would have budged. They were spent. And having got into cover, survival didn't seem to matter anymore. They just sat and stared at each other, not trusting themselves to speak. Across the field came the sound of rifle fire, shells and bombs burst in the vicinity, and there were dogfights going on above them in the sky. The tunnel amplified the noise a hundredfold. A stream of fighter planes coming in from the sea screamed past on their way to the Alban Hills. From the ditch outside there came not a sound.

Gradually, the desire to live returned. The soldiers got their legs from under the dead sergeant and warily began to study the chances of getting out of the drain at the other side of the road. They tossed who should go first. The man who lost the toss felt that perhaps they should wait a little longer, so they sat there some more and then the first man crawled out and slowly began to move away from the enemy. Each time he halted he clenched his fists with fear. He didn't dare look back. He didn't even know whether his mate was following him or not. He crawled a considerable distance before he found the courage to raise himself. His pal was behind him. Soon the two of them were running as fast as they could with their bodies close to the ground. After a little while they got more confidence and looked back. The two jeeps stood there, bodies sprawled across them, looking like a group of road workers taking a nap in the noonday sun.

The two men went back up the road that night with a burial party. They brought the corpses back and buried them the next day. What amazed them was the distance some of the men had crawled before giving up the ghost. It took a long time to find them in the dark. Several of them had gone right past the open drain, the only thing in the ditch that offered them life. Some of the fellows had never moved. The driver of the second jeep still sat there, bolt upright, his hand on the gear stick, alert, ready to move off. When they shone the hooded light on his face he stared back at them with terrible, lifeless eyes.

A little, whitewashed, ramshackle peasant farm made of plastered stone. A hard bench by an old cracked wall. A red-tiled roof, a midden in the yard, festering. A crude, makeshift door, an earthen floor where man and beast live together, a single room, low and dark, with little ventilation. Dried food hanging from the walls and the rafters, a corner to sleep, a box, a board, a bench. Low wooden partitions. A wrinkled, dark-clad, old woman sitting with her dead sow and its litter, lamenting. She wrings her hands, shrieks, screeches, screams, pulls at her white hair, and appeals to the heavens. She is past consoling. She hides her old, deeply etched face in her black skirt and howls.

But woman, have these soldiers not come as liberators of your land? Is this the way to greet those who would free you? Far better to have left you to your fate. The Germans would have taught you a lesson.

The woman is not to be consoled. She points an accusing finger at the British soldiers, she points to the picture on the wall of Christ crucified, to the heavens, then again at the soldiers. Then, she holds out her empty, deeply lined hands, cups them together, drops them in despair, and continues to lament.

What does the hag say?

The hag says that she was born of this soil, is of it, and has grown out of it. This little plot of land to which the war has come is hers. It is part of her. She will never leave it. Yet on this land all her life she has known only want. On this plain as long as she can remember through the hot summers and the cold winters she has fought a battle to survive. But it was a peaceful battle. There was no bloodshed. A wet, unyielding soil had to be coaxed and persuaded. The smallness of the holding meant an intensive, unrelenting struggle, day after day, year after year; a benumbing continuous fight, with victory always just a little beyond their grasp. Yet as a family they had always fought together. Marco and Giuseppe had been good sons. After years of toil they had bought a work horse, a great dappled gray mare, the pride of the family and the district. They had settled their married daughters nearby. They had had the joy of seeing grandchildren.

Then, woman, you have known joy as well as sorrow. Oh, why do you weep? The sow is not worth it, nor the dead litter. Where are your sons, woman?

They died under the British guns at Tobruk.

And your daughters, woman, and their children?

They are buried under that smoking hulk across the field, closer to the hills where the Germans stand.

Well, then, woman, where are your husband and the dappled gray mare?

That is my white-haired husband lying dead with his horse in the field. When my daughters' house collapsed under the fire of the great guns my husband did what any loving father would do. He leapt on his horse and went to the aid of his children. He rode out of the farmyard with the officer trying to cling to one of his legs. That is how my man rode away. I watched him go as did the others until he got halfway across the field. I could see him urging the beast on. It was then that I heard the officer give the order to fire and I watched my man fall and I ran to him and I held him until he died. It would have been far better had they shot me. Those who have killed him I have cursed and I will curse forever more.

The woman hid her head beneath her skirt again and continued to lament.

Oh, why weep, woman, oh, why weep, man? On the plain of Latium they had scratched peace and inserted the harrow of hell.

A group of British soldiers had returned to the Villa Angelina and were "standing to." They were exhausted. It was fifteen hours since the landing. Again, they peered into the darkness of the plain. Fires were burning among the ruins of several homesteads. The hills above were winking death. Sporadic shooting was going on in the darkness. Lattices of tracer fire formed and dissolved. The port of Anzio was being bombed. Ammunition was exploding. A constant stream of soldiers was passing, moving inland, shadowy figures moving along the ditches and hedgerows in single file with battle equipment and with bayonets fixed. A column of distraught civilians was being herded toward the port, the old leaning heavily upon the young. The young marched upright, a rolled blanket tied across their shoulders like Garibaldi's Thousand. A hundred yards away a wrecked fighter plane was standing on its nose in the mud, burning like a great funeral pyre, crackling and spitting.

The decisive battle had not come. On the main front in the south the Allies had suffered great casualties and had not broken through. Cassino still stood. The Liri Valley was still locked. When will the Germans come? The soldiers were confused, immensely tired. Some were told to stand down for four hours' rest. The night defenses were arranged. The soldiers stood at the back of the villa and gnawed at cold poultry bones. They ate the cocks that crowed that morning. There was some cold tea, some debilitating pack rations, and that was all. They had dug holes for themselves in the cold damp earth away from the trees and the house. When their hunger was appeased they fell into the ground and slept.

First light. This sector was still quiet. Two British soldiers were sitting in a slit trench behind the villa in the orchard, yawning. Suddenly, a pair of hands appeared over the high orchard wall. Odd! Hands! Whose hands? Then the muzzle of a rifle. Then a German helmet. German! From the direction of the sea! More hands, more Germans. A shot. The first German, now throwing his leg over the wall, fell back with a howl among his comrades. The two British soldiers raced to the villa to sound the alarm. They were disbelieved. Outflanked? From the sea? Impossible! The first Germans were running through the orchard. Sounds of a German machine pistol. The defense platoons were looking the wrong way. A mad scramble. The doors at the back of the villa were quickly slammed to. But not quickly enough. The chase was on. Upstairs and downstairs, out through one doorway, back through another, through the windows, through the orchard and the outhouses, round one corner, now round another—frantic. Crumpled khaki and field gray. The villa had its first dead.

The pace slackened. Men now stalked each other. Working from behind a chimney stack, a German began to collect rich dividends. But someone got wise to him and he suddenly came hurtling down spread-eagled off the high roof onto a group of soldiers fighting it out from behind cover in the corner of the yard. They scrambled away from the falling, screaming figure for the fear of it. A flurry of rifle fire. The chatter of light machine guns. Someone threw a grenade. A cry. The house changed hands. Now the Germans had it. A strong counterattack regained this key point. By nightfall the Germans were in possession again.

The front shifted. To enter the Villa Angelina, the soldiers no longer passed through the doorways; they used the holes in the walls. Desolation greeted the eye. The mirrors that used to stare accusingly were shattered. Broken glass and plaster lay everywhere. The carpets were covered with debris. Pictures hung drunkenly or had crashed to the floor. From one dust-covered portrait two astonished eyes peered out. Four German corpses in the kitchen awaited burial. All that could be stuffed into a pocket or a knapsack had gone.

The keyboard of the grand piano hung to the upright by one wire. Great damp and burn stains ran across the ceilings and down the walls. The roof of a bedroom had fallen in. The sky was framed in the doorway. The library had been visited by madmen. Books lay on the floor in great jumbled heaps. Whole areas were carpeted by torn pages. Mattresses lined the corridors, filthy, the sides slit open and straw scattered across the floors. Hanging over a door was a ball dress, grit- and flea-ridden. In the orchard, his back to an apple tree, sat a dead British soldier, his hands on his lap and his head thrown back as if he were sleeping off a heavy Sunday dinner.

Yet the villa still stood. So did the great trees, the dove-cote, and the well in the yard. The rooks hadn't deserted their nests. If only these uniformed bodies would go away and take their guns, and their crackling radio sets, and their chatterbox system of orders, the villa might still be restored. The core was still sound. The heart was there.

Since the Germans attacked yesterday before dawn it has been one long nightmare. There has been no rest and little food. Many of our comrades have gone. It was bitterly cold before the dawn. When the heavy barrage slackened, the mortar fire began. Soon a wedge had been driven between us and B Company; C Company had been overrun. Remnants came running back through our communication trench. They said the company had been cut to ribbons. Our orders were to go to the aid of B Company. Some of us left our positions and ran down a mud-filled track and on through a pine wood. It was three A.M. and we were chilled to the bone. There was ice on some of the evergreens. We soon came under fire and some of our fellows fell over into the mud. They crawled around in circles crying for help. We set up our mortars in a clearing and gave Jerry hell. There was not enough light to site and employ the machine guns.

The attack misfired. We attacked again. Where was B Company? Had Jerry pierced B Company as well? Good God, the runner said B Company wasn't on the right at all, they were behind us. But how could B Company be behind us, coming to our help when we were attacking on the right going to their help? There were no communications. Jerry was knocking our fellows over. Sometimes it seemed we were running alone between the trees. The attack faltered and we began to fall back. A man was hit in the thigh and went spinning around. He clung to somebody's hand. He was pulled out. The order was given to retreat. The scramble to get away was on. There was blood on the ground. Men were sprawled about as if they had just finished playing a vigorous game.

The first aid post was busy. The dead were lying outside the dugout. Wounded were being carried in. A man with faltering steps arrived with a comrade on his back.

7

Through my fingers I can see Father Cantimore's laced-up boots. Carlotta and Giovanni are kneeling beside a great bundle of clothes. Around us are the walls of the big cellar. I didn't know that any place except the church could be so big. Mamma says that the institute is the biggest building in the whole of Latium. Look at the cracks that run up the wall and across the ceiling. It's like a spider's web. How awful to be a spider and live in this dark hole without windows. I've never seen such large pillars. You could play hide-and-seek round them. The old people are propped against the wall. They had to be carried down the steps. I wish Father Cantimore would keep still. He is throwing great spooky shadows on the wall. Mamma says I should not grind my teeth, but I am so cold. I am afraid of the darkness.

Why do people cry so loud? I've never seen our *pastore* cry before. I wish Nonna were here, but Nonna is in Rome. Mamma says the war has come to the village.

Father Cantimore says we must have trust and *pazienza*. We must not forget our Mater Dolorosa. He is reciting the De Profundis for those who have fallen asleep in the Kiss of the Lord. "Addormentarsi nel bacio del Signore." I ask Mamma why we say the De Profundis so much now. She says it is the war. I wonder what the war is. Carlotta's sister fell asleep during the night in the Kiss of the Lord. I said every word of the Salve Regina. They say the sun is shining upstairs. Why is it so dark down here?

The war came to the village when we were all fast asleep. Mamma shook me and told me that we must run to the institute to hide from the war. Mamma carried Marco and Carlo. We ran across the field in the night. My blanket is dirty from the field. I am glad the war has come because now I will see Papa. Papa has been with the war in a desert. Now he will be here too. I like my Papa.

I have never seen Mamma so frightened before. She screamed. She made me frightened, too. We all screamed. But I wasn't frightened running across the field. I've never run across the field in the middle of the night before. Mamma kept dropping things, but she would not let me stop to pick them up. The sky was full of fireworks. Great red lights, green lights, hundreds of candles floating down. Titino didn't mind the war coming to the village. He's seen fireworks before. And he's a very brave cat. He can kill the largest rat. When we ran from our cottage Titino followed us across the field. I know because once I fell over him. I couldn't find him when I got to the institute. There was such a crowd. A man knocked me away from the big door. Mamma called him a devil and a pig. He must be very bad to be a devil and a pig. I wonder if Titino has found any food. I wonder if they've put the fire out in Bernadelli's cottage. Mamma says not to ask so many questions. Perhaps Papa will come soon.

It is cold here and my knees hurt. At home we have a mat to kneel on when we say the Rosary. Father Cantimore says we shall all go back to the village when the soldiers have passed. Carlotta says they are going to Rome to capture the Pope. Perhaps they will take the train. Father Cantimore is going upstairs to ask when we can all go home.

The grown-ups say it is night again. The men brought us some pasta, some candles, and more clothing. Why do they look so frightened? I was glad they found my white frock. Some of the women tried to light a fire to warm us. The smoke was so bad that they had to put it out again. One of the men made *zuppa* upstairs with all the guns firing. It wasn't good *zuppa* but we ate it quickly. Papa has not come. Mamma has told us lots of stories. She made us all laugh, playing with us. When we can have the lantern we play but we do not run away from the light. The old pedlar man gave Carlotta and me a needle and thread and buttons and scissors. We always wanted to know what he carried in his box through the village. Now we know. We are allowed to choose our own ribbons. Carlotta and I have tied ribbons in our hair. Mamma says the pedlar man is a holy and a good man. She says long ago he was like Father Cantimore. Once

I went across the field to Carlotta's farm in the early evening. And we went into the kitchen and knelt down on the stone flags with Carlotta's family and said the Rosary together. It was the pedlar man who led us in prayer. At Carlotta's they put sand on their kitchen floor and it makes your knees itch.

The noises outside grow louder. The whole cellar fills with dust. It is very difficult for the old ones to breathe. One of them has fallen asleep in the Lord and is carried beyond the light of the lantern into the darkness. Dust falls from the ceiling. A man tells us that Father Cantimore will not come back. The old pedlar man is saying another De Profundis with the villagers.

There is a lot of shouting and running about upstairs. Several villagers stand at the top of the stairs to stop the war from coming into the cellar. I ask Mamma why the ceiling jumps? She says it's the guns. I ask her, Shall we see Papa soon? She doesn't answer but tells her beads. I wonder if she is frightened again. She draws us closer.

The men on the stairs say that the *tedeschi* have gone. But we must stay still and quiet. An *inglese* comes down the cellar steps. He is in a great hurry. He carries a lamp that can reach the far end of the cellar wall. He says that we must go away in a ship. Some of the villagers begin to cry. Why can't they go home? they ask. Everyone makes ready to leave. Only one lantern burns now. The villagers crowd the cellar steps sitting on their little bundles. The sick and the old have been carried up and put near the door. The potatoes have been shared and we eat them. Mamma wraps up Marco and Carlo until you can only see their faces. The old pedlar man says he will help us. The villagers gnaw their potatoes and weep.

We wait. Mamma falls asleep and then jumps. She holds Marco and Carlo. I sit against them. Mamma says I must hang on to her hand and never let go.

Mamma is shaking me. "Come, come quickly," she says. It is time to go to the ship. The lantern is at the foot of the stairs. The war is still here. The pedlar man is with us. Mamma takes my hand. I promise not to let go. We hurry up the stairs.

An *inglese* stands at the top. *"Presto, presto,"* he says. The sky is lit with flashes. There is a large truck in the yard with a cover over the roof. Arms reach down to pull us in. Carlotta is calling. I am very frightened. Carlo has already been passed into the truck. Mamma bends down to pick me up. There is a great flash of blinding light.

The lantern is still on the stone cellar steps casting its shadows on the wall. The pedlar man is wiping my face and calling to me gently. Where are Marco and Carlo and Mamma? Have they gone to the ship without us? I cry for my Mamma. The pedlar man tells us they are coming very soon.

"Very soon," he says.

I cannot stop crying. He has had an accident. There is blood all over his face and shirt. He cannot stand up properly. I ask him to take me home. He shakes his head.

"Soon," he says, "soon."

He is weeping.

The lantern has burned low. I can see the old pedlar man propped against the pillar, sleeping, with his head down. I am glad he is here. He will take me home. I call out to him. He does not answer. I reach over and touch him. He topples over. I call out to him again. He does not answer. He is very cold. I think he is sleeping in the Lord. I must go home without him. I don't think he will come to our village again with his little box of things. Last time he came to our cottage he gave me two little wooden dolls that jumped up and down on the end of a stick.

The war is still upstairs. I can hear the soldiers. They are still smashing glass. I will tell the soldiers I am here. I will tell them I am Bernadette Sapori and that I want to go to my Mamma. I didn't let go of Mamma's hand. She must have let go of mine.

8

I'm Fred Topsom. I come from Poplar in East London. Started out playing Boy Scouts with the good old territorials. Came serious stuff with Jerry and I found myself in the old Black Cat London Division. Good mob. Since then we've had everything sewn on our sleeves: cats, bears, fists, lumps of cheese. Made no difference to the fighting. You don't fight with your sleeve.

Seen a lot since the Western Desert. Don't like what we are in now. Landing was all right. Piece of cake. But the book says, "Take the high ground." Instead, we're sinking deeper into the mud. There's a mountain in front of us and the sea at our back. This beats all the rules. The answer is, of course, don't *stand* there and gripe: take the high ground. But I ask you, how do you take the high ground when you haven't got what it takes to take it?

God knows we tried. But you cannot beat Jerry by bluffing him. Unless you're ready to give him an overwhelming punch on the nose once you've got him bluffed. But here we bluff him and then expect Jerry to go home. Jerry doesn't do that. Look what we did at Campoleone. Stuck our neck out there all right, we did. Lost half our mob. Supposed to meet "light covering forces." Instead what do we do? We go slap bang into the 29th Panzer-Grenadier Regiment. Now those fellows are known for their sharp teeth. Seen nothing of the blokes that were to take Cassino and come on. They say there's been no breakthrough. They say the Yanks jumped across the Rapido and got the chopper bad.

This has been one hell of a week. Jump off, dig, fight, lick, bury your dead. Then jump off, dig, fight, lick, and bury your dead again. Then back to where you started. Now jump off again. This time in the dark. *Bang, wallop, bang.* Jerry doesn't like us. Now Jerry has been told to jump off. Now Sarge says we have to jump back. Now Jerry jumps back. Now we jump off again. Now Jerry jumps off, too. In six days we've taken prisoners from eight different divisions. There's no sense in this. It's like the old snakes-and-ladders game we used to play. Yesterday we moved before our turn and our gunners shelled us instead of Jerry.

And what a godforsaken place this is. A few trees, a few measly farmhouses. The rest is bog, bush, and water. And look at the grub. We're surviving on what we can scrounge and Yank pack rations. Dammit, it's a wonder we haven't lost the war eating that Yank stuff. It's all wrapping and bull. When you've swallowed the spearmint and the fags and the glucose candy and the dehydrated muck that goes with it, your guts feel empty. Gives you wind, it does. It's got nothing on British treacle and duff. Anything that makes a noise and can be eaten around here was knocked off in the first few days. We've the Dukes on our left. Dukes are known for clearing the grub out of a place in no time. Big eaters, the Dukes.

Here we go again. Sarge says we are going to jump off. The fellow who put us in this damned plain ought to be made to jump off with us. Hope we get out of this snakes-and-ladders game soon. Let's shake the dice hard and try for a six. We'll need a lot of sixes to get up these hills.

I'm Franklin S. Holtzinger, Jr. I belong to the 1st Ranger Battalion. I'm a GI, a "government issue" soldier—everybody's dog. I fight the war on my feet with a rifle and a bayonet.

My outfit was at Salerno. A mighty close thing that Salerno business. I remember that all too well. Wally and I (Wally was my buddy) were creeping up trying to work round a nasty Kraut who just wasn't smart enough to get the hell out of it.

"Frankie," Wally said, "when you leave this ditch you're going to win the Purple Heart." Well, we never did leave that ditch. At least not the way Wally intended.

"Come on," I says to Wally, "let's go and burn that Kraut out of there."

But Wally never budged. He just lay there with his head on the bank where we'd taken cover from some Kraut fire. I thought he was kidding.

"What is it, Wally?" I said, and then I noticed he'd got a nasty little hole through his helmet just above his ear. Then I guess I must have forgotten what we're supposed to do when things like that happen. Hell, Wally and I had come a long way together. We'd fought together, grubbed together, and bedded together. We led the basketball team for three years straight at Kalamazoo. Dated the girls together.

"What the hell do you think you're doing?" said Sarge when he came down the ditch.

"I'm sitting with Wally," I said. "Wally's dead. Wally's mom's going to be awful upset."

"Jesus," Sarge said.

Well, the war wasn't the same without Wally. This bum thing we're on here at Anzio makes no difference one way or other. Nothing's gone right since Wally went. We lands here in the dark, everybody freezing cold. We wins a canal. Then we loses a canal. Then we wins the canal back again. Then it's daylight and we have to dig, dig, dig, or die. These Krauts are everywhere. Radio said we had caught the Krauts napping. Well, there were enough stiffs on the beach. And if this is the Krauts asleep, what happens, I says to Private Kassori (First Class), when the Krauts wake up?

Brother, did they wake up! For one whole week I've been wishing myself back in Kalamazoo. Should have stayed and done my senior year, like Dad said. These Krauts don't sleep. And they won't let us wash, either. We pumped water from the canal and rigged up a hot shower. But every time anyone stripped off and went in, the Krauts would fire on it. The boys dashed out with their white tails bobbing across the field.

"A fellow deserves all he gets once he steps out of his pants," said Sarge.

Sarge is from Georgia. He's still fighting the Civil War. He has a pet hate: Sherman tanks. "That son of a bitch Sherman!"

Then, as if we didn't have enough to worry about, Lieutenant Fetcher comes on the scene.

"See that little place at the foot of the hills?" he says, pointing to Cisterna. "Well, look, you and me, we're going to take that place from the Krauts."

Well, everybody knows we never did. They got us to Cisterna all right. They took us in the night along ditches, through enemy positions, past enemy sentries. When the light came I could have picked up a stone and hit it. But then the Krauts spotted us—all twelve hundred of us.

"This is it," said Lieutenant Fetcher. "Let's go!"

Well, we didn't go; we never got off first base.

"Go! go! go!" said the colonel over the radio.

But how do you go, Colonel, when those who go drop dead? We were climbing over our own men. It didn't take us long to realize we were trapped—dead trapped. They gave us the lot, the whole nine yards: self-propelled guns, machine guns, mortars, snipers. There we were, surrounded, in a treeless plain, without cover.

The end came about noon when enemy tanks came out of Cisterna down the road to Isola Bella. The tanks raced among us, driving us out of our shallow holes and herding us into small groups for destruction. The order was given to scatter. But by then it was too late. Kraut hit the jackpot that day. It's the day my Regimental Combat Team died. Out of seven hundred and sixty-seven men, six of us escaped. Lot of boys from Kalamazoo. Out of a total of twelve hundred that went out, four hundred of us fought our way back. We were sort of quiet when we got back into shelter. What burned us up bad was to see our buddies trying to fight their way through to us. Did all and more than any man can expect, but instead of pulling us out they got smacked on the nose for their trouble. Kraut knew what he was doing. He trapped them as he trapped us. A lot of good boys died trying to help us. They say the boys on the southern front met the same fate crossing the Rapido, only worse. The lieutenant and the sergeant died. Lieutenant said that if we grabbed Cisterna, we could soon grab Rome. But I don't know what we want to grab Rome for. This is a kind of mixed-up war. Here I am, coming from the oldest German family in town, killing Krauts. Boy, how mixed up can you get? If this is Europe, then the Krauts can keep it. I'd tell my senator that.

A long thin face. Splashes of blood. It is very close. It is choking me.

"Alles wohl . . . Schlaf . . . Your Krieg ist beendet, soldier . . . beendet . . . Krieg beendet . . . alles wohl."

But all is not well. The Englishman's face has become as thin and as flat as a plate. I am slipping into a pit. Who am I and what am I? I am without hope. I am lost.

I must have slept. I am numb and cold. I cannot feel my left side at all.

"You all right?"

Another face bends over me.

"Want a smoke?"

"*Wasser*," I say, "water."

Someone moistens my lips and goes away.

Two or three figures stand around me, muttering. They turn to the others lying alongside me.

I can move my head. On my left is a Negro. Momentarily, our eyes meet. There is only fear and apprehension. Beyond the Negro is a *Feldwebel* lying unconscious. On my right is a British officer. There is a red beribboned hat on his bed. He is lying motionless, like a corpse, staring at the ceiling. Beyond him is an American soldier. He notices me looking around.

"You're out of the war," he calls.

I try to smile.

"You're in a hospital ship third-class, bud," he says. "Must get the hell out of here soon or the Krauts will be on us. We're anchored at the spot where the Krauts sank a hospital ship a few days ago."

He doesn't know he is talking to a German.

I reply in broken English. The American is surprised but is eager to talk. He tells me he is from Illinois.

I try to tell him something about myself. I am Fritz Steingarten. I am twenty-three. I come from Kochel on the Kochelsee in Upper Bavaria, from a small pasture farm at the foot of the mountains. I was a *Gefreiter* in the 29th Panzer-Grenadier Regiment. The British must have picked me up on the battlefield. I can remember a blinding flash. Nothing more.

It is too much of an effort to talk. There is a strong smell of disinfectant and ether. Some men have had emergency surgery. As they come out of the ether they moan like wounded animals. They are working on a man behind me. He lows like the cows in the stables in winter waiting to be fed. The British officer has just fished out his hat from underneath his stretcher, where an orderly had put it. Perhaps the army is all that he has. A life slips away. The body is taken out. Another man is quickly brought in to fill the empty cot.

At the end of the ship's deck is a great opening through which I can see the bright sky. A German fighter plane shoots across, followed by puffs of gray and black smoke from anti-aircraft fire. Brave pilot. He fights almost alone in the sky. It must be freezing by the door. There are sounds of battle in the distance. An English soldier plays a mouth organ. Next to him a man sobs quietly.

The door is closed, the anchor has been raised, the engines are beginning to throb. Now the ship is under way. The only light we have comes from the swinging lamps above our heads. It's like lying in a great steel chest.

I am still numb down my left side. The Negro has never spoken. The orderlies move from one soldier to another.

They have just thrown a cloth over the *Feldwebel*'s face. They will bury him now at sea.

Where have I been? Cassino? Cassino was a long time ago . . . November, December, and January. I remember nothing but fighting—hard grueling fighting; desperate fighting with now sweat, now blood, now tears running through the dirt covering one's face. I cannot remember Christmas. Fighting, bombardment, fighting, bombardment, crouching, running, digging, praying. On the ground the fear of sudden death. Below the ground the fear of being buried alive. It cannot have been true. But it was true. When you were not fighting you slept with your kit on, with your rifle frozen to your hand, and fear in your heart, and you froze, and the food froze, and your frostbitten hands suppurated, and the *Trommelfeuer* was incessant. One by one, day by day, they went. Some I could hold and comfort as they passed on; others I never saw. They just went. And these were great big fellows. Fellows from Kochel, some of them. Where are the boys with whom I sailed on the lake? Where are those who one summer not very long ago rowed up the Königsee with me to St. Bartholomä? Did we not drink and make merry together? The steep hills echoed our laughter. Don't you remember the echo of the bugle from the mountains, remote, pure, and mystical? Where are those fellows from Kochel? The fellows who sat round the great tiled stove at home and yarned. They can't all have gone. But they have. They have found a resting place at Cassino. I am the only one left from Kochel.

Cassino? Cassino? Yes, I remember. When the reinforcements came we didn't believe them. They had been promised so often. Since December our lines of communication to Rome had been under attack by the partisans; troop trains had been derailed, supplies destroyed. One night down the Liri Valley an ammunition train had exploded with a thunderous roar. When eventually the reinforcements came they had to help us out of the line. We were half dead. Some of us became hysterical—first crying, then laughing. They took us out of shellfire, down the Liri Valley, along the twisting road to Frosinone, and there we collapsed in a barn. We did not care whether we wakened again.

Then came the alarm! The enemy had landed on our flank at Anzio! They shook us and shook us. The enemy was pouring ashore. And the defense troops? They have just replaced you at Cassino. Yes! Hurry, hurry, hurry! For God's sake hurry while there is still time. Never mind which regiment you belong to—fight as Germans. Hurry, or they'll cut our forces in two.

I cannot remember the rest. I must have fought for several days, but where? Where have I been?

The thump of the ship's engines. The lamps swinging above my head, backward and forward. Now with halos of rainbow light around them. Shells, noise, numbness, thirst.

Do you remember Kochelsee covered in mist, and the calls echoing in the hills? I must live. I must go back; without comrades, but I can tell them what the others did. No! I cannot do that; silence is better. I must avoid their eyes. How can I tell them of a life gone, that was unique, all, now and forever? Nor can I tell them that I have seen man the killer and God-man the redeemer and that I have looked upon the face of a man who went out to die for a man.

If I go home I shall go with a new love of the intimate little things of life, a new hate of words and messianic man. The big things for which we said we would die have passed like a forest fire, leaving nothing but desolation in their wake. All spent. Look upon this sea of broken bodies. The intimate little things remain. The sight of mountain flowers gently shaking their colored heads in the breeze, the sheen of meadow grass yielding to the wind, the pitch of the farm roof at home. Little things. Do you remember a staircase of a large department store in Munich? How long ago? Watching the assistants take down the cheap pictures of Christ and His Apostles and use the same nails to hang the portraits of Germany's political leaders. And the crowds running upstairs and downstairs, pushing us aside, not caring, snatching. And I wondered why my father was so moved!

They have come to take the *Feldwebel* away.

9

He came to us when we were resting in an olive grove in Tunisia. He came at night, through the trees and past the bivouacs, carrying a swagger cane. A little lean, hard, dark, intense figure with a pencil mustache, ducking his head underneath the branches as he made his way purposefully to the CO's tent. A servant followed him heavily laden. He'd never seen action until he joined us. What he had seen in his forty years of life had caused his honest face to take upon itself an expression of slight astonishment. It was rather a disapproving look and it never left him.

When we first saw him he was as clean as a new pin. From his hat to his shoes you couldn't fault him. He was actually wearing a tie. As a regular officer coming from an army family, he was obviously delighted to join a battle-tried unit such as ours. However, the way in which we were all lying and slipping and slopping about under the trees, in every state of undress, trying to shake off the dirt and the memories of our last action, had caught him unawares. Perhaps, that's what caused him to react to our questions with a good deal of reserve. The more charitable among us interpreted his initial stiffness as that of the self-conscious new boy out to do his best. The less charitable at once dubbed him "Crusty-Arse," and the name stuck.

Before we could stop him Crusty had ducked his head under the flap of the CO's tent, swagger cane and all, and had come smartly to attention at the CO's table, which stood against his bed. "Major Chancellor from England, sir, reporting." On the bed, sitting cross-legged, his bare legs sticking out from the nightshirt he was wearing, was a figure reminiscent of a nineteenth-century Algerian bey. Had Major Chancellor entered the wrong tent? No. This scruffy-looking pedlar from the bazaars sitting among a pile of washing picking threads off a sock was indeed the CO, a battle-hardened commanding officer, shorn of all illusions about man and war—a "do-it-yourselfer" up from the ranks, the hard way. Secretly, we had hoped that the shock might cause Crusty to fall backward into the steaming bath that the old man was about to indulge in, but it didn't. The slightly disapproving look remained.

And when the old man had asked his stock question of new arrivals—not "And how are things at home?" or "Did you have a pleasant journey?" but "What is your favorite book and why?"—Crusty had hardly blinked. "*Wind in the Willows*," he'd answered, to our astonishment, without a moment's hesitation. *Wind in the Willows* for a forty-year-old crusty regular officer aching for active service! Why? Well, because . . . and then he'd gone off into a long discussion of the author's use of animals to express human characterization, a discussion that soon palled on the ears of the Algerian bey, especially as he watched his bathwater cool.

Crusty was not easily floored. As the new second-in-command he gave his first unpopular order that evening.

"Sergeant major, companies will parade for P.T. at six A.M."

"I beg your pardon, sir, the commanding officer's view on physical training is—"

"I'm not asking you to tell me what the CO's view is, sergeant major, I'm giving you an order. You will see that it is carried out."

"Very good, sir."

An olive grove of cursing soldiers, still in every state of undress, bending and heaving in the early-morning light. Hungry mosquitoes making the most of the opportunity.

Anzio. A hideout at the side of a railway bed. Seven months had passed. The road from the olive grove in Tunisia via Sicily and southern Italy had been long and hard. Along that road Crusty had upheld the high traditions of the British Army. But he had never lost his stiffness, his personal insecurity.

A tattered, mud-covered figure came down the railway line, exhausted, but home.

"In heaven's name," you'd said, "It's Fog."

Five days ago he had spoken to you on his portable radio while men were killing each other around him.

"I'm closing down now," he'd said. "Is there any last message?"

"None, Sugar Baker One," you'd said. "None, other than good luck. Roger and out."

And then, slowly, you'd pulled the earphones off your head, and you'd held them before you on your knee, and you'd stared at them, and listened and prayed and hoped and then you'd brought your fist down on the radio set in front of you with such force that you'd dented the metal and caused your hand to bleed. And now, here was Fog home again.

Fog in Crusty's dugout, reporting.

"You did what!" Crusty said to Fog. The disapproving look was still there.

"I dropped the set and made a run for it," said Fog.

"You abandoned your equipment," said Crusty. "Do you realize, corporal, that's like saying you threw away your rifle?"

"Well, it was either the set or me," said Fog.

"Corporal," said Crusty, "you'll go back for that radio set tonight. Nobody will abandon equipment without orders in this unit as long as I am second-in-command. You'll go back for it tonight, corporal. That's an order!"

Fog saluted with his heels and tottered out of the dugout.

"He can't do it, mate. He daren't do it. He'd have the

battalion up in arms. We'll go and see Sarge, and Sarge will see the sergeant major, who'll see the CO."

Sergeant Major saw Crusty.

"Now, sir, for the life of a comrade there isn't one of us here who wouldn't take a chance. But for a piece of metal? Why, sir, we haven't enough men to go chasing across the battlefield like that after broken equipment."

"If a piece of metal was all that was at stake, sergeant major, I would say no more. But there is something more at stake here—regimental honor."

"Begging your pardon, sir, but most of us are proud members of the regiment by necessity, not by choice. To these men the thing that matters is a life."

"The order still stands."

Sergeant major went direct to the CO. Whom should the CO uphold? A fine pickle!

"Let the order stand, but send out a patrol. Patrols have to go out anyway; if they bring in the equipment everybody's happy."

"But everybody is already happy except Major Chancellor, and besides, there is no patrol work to be done in the area where the corporal abandoned the radio set."

"The order still stands."

"Take it to Brigade, mate, and Division. Write to your Member of Parliament."

"How can you, man, in this short time. They'll think Fog's mutinous. Somebody who is responsible for something has given an order. He's been upheld by his commanding officer. What is there to take to Division?"

"Tell Fog to go sick—battle fatigue."

"He refuses."

"But this is murder. We are sending a tired man into danger for no other reason than somebody's pigheadedness."

"Look, stop getting excited and sentimental about a life. Lives are lost all the time."

"The order still stands."

Dusk. A small patrol left the railway bed and headed for the front.

"Orders are orders."

"I hope for Crusty's sake," said one of the sullen observers, "that Fog comes back."

Dawn.

"The patrol's back but Fog's not with it."

"That's done it. We don't want the details. The bastard killed him. Of course, others have been killed in the night. We're not denying that. We're saying Fog needn't have been killed and he didn't have a chance."

Crusty continued to look slightly surprised. All men avoided him. No one went near him unless he was forced to. If he approached a man or a group of men they dispersed at once. If he cornered a man in a slit trench the man refused to look up. He could have put the whole battalion on a charge for "dumb insolence." No one spoke to him. The sergeant major went sick. The senior sergeant asked to be posted away from Crusty's side. Crusty only had to speak on a radio network and it fell silent. If junior officers had to sit with him, they sat apart. The look on Crusty's face never changed.

*　*　*

Crusty, in the command vehicle. A heavy shell scraped the roof. For a moment those inside ceased to breathe. They studied the floor of the vehicle and were limp and empty. If the trajectory of the shell had been an inch or two lower! Crusty, his face twitching, turned to the radio operator: "I want you to sing 'You Are My Sunshine,' " he said, "and that's an order."

The operator opened his mouth and then shut it again. Sarge slipped out to bring the CO.

Crusty's gone, God help him. They took him down the railway line singing to himself, sadly. He still looked surprised and slightly disapproving of what he saw. He came to us with such high hopes. Can't think why some of us treated Crusty as we did. We're going to miss Crusty.

10

How many days have passed? Is it weeks? We have given up counting; we have given up thinking; we only move and act. Another dusk. We look out from our hole and watch the gold of the sunset across the sea turn to gray and gray to black. The low clouds in the west lose their warmth and their color and then are gone. Today was to be a decisive day, but like all the other decisive days that have come and gone it has only been decisive in robbing us of some of our comrades. The war goes on unchanged. We don't have our full heart in the game. Neither side has the strength to knock the other side out of the beachhead. It's enough that we're alive and no one took our hole while we were away.

What can we remember of the day? Blurred images. Visions. Shapes. The forming up in the dark. The dread of being starkly outlined by enemy flares. Crawling forward at first light. The dampness of the plain. The tufts of coarse grass scratching your face. A beetle scurrying away from under your nose. Green shoots of wheat. A drop of dew on a stalk sparkling like a diamond in the risen sun. Strange creatures crawling along on either side of you, some carrying wire cutters and bangalore torpedoes, ready to drive a hole through the shell-torn wire. The arm signal to stay, wait. The cold damp earth. The beginning of the barrage. The coming of a great Allied air armada. We count them, one hundred, two hundred, three hundred . . . the most terrifying bombing of German positions. A plane turning over and over in flames. Others thunder onward in massive formations, their wings glinting in the morning sun. Parachutists floating down to earth between the black puffs of anti-aircraft fire. The whole earth shaking and trembling. Great soundwaves rising from the ground, like a rainbow, ungodly, wicked. A German voice on a neighboring frequency. A German voice losing control of itself. Why had the anti-aircraft batteries ceased to fire? the German general of artillery demanded. A pathetic answer: Because, Herr General, the gunners are dead. Now bombing without any retaliation. The Luftwaffe casually brushed aside by countless fighters. Slow, leisurely, meticulous, scientific, murderous bombing. Not just destructive—senseless. Great ladders of bombs slithering down the sky. Giant clouds of dust and flame. More shelling. As the vast air armada disappears above the hills, a stunned silence fills the land. Nothing moves. Nothing stirs. All is strangely still and quiet. The world is empty. A time when words would have no meaning.

Now the order to attack. Through the dust and the smoke

and the dirt. The first objectives overrun and occupied. Many dead Germans. Many live Germans, ashen-faced, taut, terrified, crawling out of the rubble and the ground, trying to raise their arms, unable to raise their heads, shocked and tottery, like a man recovering from a stroke. Now, a counterattack. Now get out. Now go back. Noise. Smoke. Shoutings. Clatter. Frightened, bewildered eyes. Terror. Death.

He was the last German to be winkled out of a machine-gun pit. The Germans had fought to the bitter end, gloriously; one man left, no weapons. We told him to get the hell out of it fast, and no ruddy nonsense. We were tired and nervous. "Put your hands up, brother, and keep them there. You're the lucky one," we said. But the young German boy with his dead comrades lying around him didn't intend to be "the lucky one." As we covered him with our guns he suddenly tore his shirt open and bared his hairy chest. Then like an animal at bay he hurled defiance at us, shouting, "Sieg Heil! Sieg Heil! Sieg Heil!" Not another word did he say. We didn't know what to do. We stood gawking at him. "Good mind to knock the cocky bastard off," one of the fellows said, but everyone knew he didn't mean it. We didn't do that sort of thing to men who fought like that. Well, not until this occasion we hadn't. Then from behind came the rattle of a submachine gun. The German boy collapsed upon his dead comrades, dragging his face down the sharp jutting shale edge of the trench. Blessedly, one burst was enough. There was no shrieking and groveling at our feet. Thank goodness nobody else had asked to be executed like that. Death was common enough, but not that kind of death.

Lying exhausted in a hole. A squadron of British tanks was coming up in support. The commander calmly directed the battle using cricket parlance: "Harry, I'd like you to go a little farther out in the field in the hope of a long catch . . . Charlie, would you move over to silly mid-off . . . Now Bryant what about you trying to take a cheeky single . . . I'll long stop . . ." and so it went on.

We might have been at Lords in London watching Test cricket on a warm sunny afternoon and wondering whether the tea break was far away. Suddenly, across the squadron leader's voice came a sharp ominous click. We'd heard it before. We couldn't see the tank but we knew what the click meant. Charlie took over the radio network. The others obeyed his orders calmly, resolutely, as if it were the most natural thing in the world for their comrade to depart suddenly like that—with a click as adieu.

Human sacrifice had not changed the day. It was dusk and we were back where we started. Except there were stretchers lying everywhere bearing the wounded and the dead.

A man got up from the side of a stretcher where he'd been coaxing a pal to hang on to life. The pal meant to hang on to life, too. It was dear to him. He had hardly tasted the joys of it. But look how the face had shrunk and the skin had become taut over the cheeks and the nose.

"He's gone all right, mate."

For a moment, the man who had just got up looked

around, lost, despairing, then he took a running kick at an empty bully beef tin lying on the ground.

"What a bloody war this is," he said.

Yes, for some this had been a decisive day. They said that tomorrow some of us would go farther back for a wash, a hot meal, and a chance to dry out our clothing.

11

There had been rumors for days. Now there it was in black and white. There could be no arguing:

"Beginning at 0200 hours the 12th Brigade will hand over its sector of the front to units of the 18th Brigade. The main body of the 12th Brigade will proceed to the staging area (map reference) and will embark from the port of Anzio under directions from the military port authorities on the same day. The Brigade will proceed to the rear area of the Army Group for rest and re-forming."

The operation order from Division went on to deal with routes, order of march, axis, command, emplacements, re-placements, sick and wounded, supplies, and a hundred other things. But you're not interested in the "hundred other things," are you? You're quivering and trembling at the thought of escaping from the bridgehead at all. Two things occupy your mind: Can you somehow survive the next forty-eight hours, and if you do survive, is it not possible that you might leave behind you forever this damp, dank, cold, rotting lump of earth where death can come so swiftly, and so violently? The pity if this strange land becomes your nemesis at this late hour. Your roots run into another soil far away. The fate of this broken land and its suffering people does not concern you. You dare not let it concern you. You came to fight and destroy. Now you would willingly slip away from it all. You've had your fill. Gladly would you turn your back on all this, for the shame of it.

0200 hours. Dark, but starlit. Long columns of men are making their way back from the front. Equally long columns are making their way into the line. The men move like ghosts. There is no noise, except for the squelch of mud and the jingle of equipment. The men going out are too exhausted to talk; the men filing into the trenches and dugouts are too apprehensive to make conversation. The situation is too tense and desperate for chatter. Yet there are odd snatches.

"Good luck, mate."

"It's all yours."

"Keep the place tidy and warm now."

"Don't forget to water the flowers."

"If you have to leave put the key under the mat."

The sounds die, the bodies continue to file in and out. Those coming know they have been drawn to the center of the web of war. Those going are desperate to break out, to get away. Except for the odd burst of shellfire the front is relatively quiet.

The stream of men continues to pour toward the shore. Will you make it? Jerry will start something, he will. Just like Jerry. Peevish bastard, him. You have one foot out of the grave now. Poor sods, Jerry would say. They think they're going to get away with it but they're not. Oh, no. And Jerry would bash you over the head. That's it, you'll never escape from this hole. You're doomed to stay and die here. The hellfire of war has already changed you. There isn't any getting away from it now. You'll always stay here. You're a child of war. You are not you. "You" has gone for always. You'll wake up soon and be back there in the filth again, looking through the wire, shivering, with your feet frozen and your teeth chattering and the hail and the snow pelting down on your face. Oh, no. You're not going to get away with it. You're going to stand there with your boots sinking lower and lower into the mud—waiting, and worrying, and staring, and listening, and ducking, and running, and weeping from fear and despair and frustration and anger and sorrow, with your nerves on edge forever.

No, it must be real. That was Sarge telling you to get a ruddy move on or, by God, he'd give the order "About turn"! Sarge knows that most of you are licked. You've been too long in the line. He can tell it the way you hold your heads. Soon the reaction will set in. Once you fellows flop down on your arses you'll never shift. Orders are no good when a man's half dead. Once you are dry and warm and no longer have the fear of being overrun and slain you will sleep and sleep and sleep. What else do you ask? Only to survive and sleep.

"Keep moving there! Come on now, Shorty, no straggling. Come on now, come on now, down the ditches, across the fields, past the rows of guns lying quiet and sinister and ready to do mischief, past the vehicles all burned out and smelling of death, past the tanks still burning from gunfire."

All right, so be it, these stars are the same stars that Caesar saw. Stars and men never change. But watch the shelling. Can't get knocked off now. What the hell is holding up the column in front?

This is the corner where Tiny copped it. Couldn't believe it. Why does a man get knocked off like that? It's cheating, that's what it is. The old reaper, cheating. Tiny was sitting on the jeep bonnet, talking. A shell fell too far away even to notice. But Tiny slid off the bonnet onto the road.

"Come on, Tiny," you said, "get up, you old loafer." Tiny never got up anymore.

"Poor devil hasn't got any lungs," said the Doc when you took Tiny back. "There isn't a squeak in him."

"But we were talking to him."

The Doc shrugged his shoulders and turned away.

Tiny was a genius. He could make any noise you liked. Take off a Jerry; take off the British general with a pebble in his mouth. Proper skit, Tiny was. His favorite was the London tube. Fair made the Cockneys cry, he did. Shut your eyes and there you were underneath Piccadilly with the tube engine throbbing away impatiently, and the doors hissing and clanging as they opened and shut, and the noise of the crowd, and the call of the porters. He was a genius, Tiny was. Last general was too much for Tiny. Used to call his poor sods of soldiers "my army" as if they were fighting for him.

"Mister," Tiny would say, taking off his old mum speaking to the general, "if you fink that my ole man an me 'ave rised ar Tiny ter fite for you, cor, y've got another fink comin'. Y'av'."

As Tiny used to say, "A'm fiten for 'Ackney Wick, South'nd, and Watney's Pile Ile. Wot yer fiten fo, mite?"

Proper genius, Tiny. Nobody learned him anything. That's the head of Tiny's black cat sticking out of Toby's knapsack. Squad wouldn't part with Tiny's cat. We used to have a calf, too, but we ate him when St. Anthony wasn't looking. This is the corner where Tiny copped it. Big fire on here. Didn't think there was anything left to burn. Keep moving. There are showers of sparks falling across you. This is no place to stand around and wait for orders.

Thank God, the column's underway again. See that big storm drain running under the road over there? On D+I it was crammed tight with Italian women and children. Women across whose faces ran the deep furrows of work and worry and sorrow. Like a lot of black currants stuffed in a box. Crammed it was to the very edge. How did they breathe? Don't know. Well, with shells falling on both sides of the road it's kind of dangerous to be jammed in a drain. Especially when it's not your war. Jerry puts a heavy on the doorstep and, phew, you're all dead. Damn the order about civilians being told to stay put; "frozen," according to staff bumpf.

"Signora," you said, "here multo pericolo. Go to the *mare*, go to the sea, the sea, boats, escape, safety. Oh, hell, what's 'safety' in Italian?"

A young signora, raven-black hair protruding from her

scarf, the darkest shining eyes, great brass earrings hanging down to her shoulders, smiles shyly, and edges back into the drain, clinging to her child.

"Try again."

"Signora, signora . . . oh, look luv, don't be daft, if you don't grab your kid and run for it you're both going to get killed."

"Why not pull her out and kick her down the road?"

The smile has gone. She bites.

"Leave the bitch!" Did they survive? A black Madonna with a child in black, stuffed in a drain, surrounded by other women who wore their black shawls like hoods clutched across the throat.

Black, always black. Black. Have you ever looked down into the black hole of a cellar of an Italian house from the street level, in the middle of the night, and called out to ask if anyone was there before you threw a grenade in, and the echo of your voice came back to mock you, and there was stillness, and just when you were ready to pull the pin and let the grenade go, to make sure, an enormous noise rose from the bowels of the earth and these same black-clad, hooded women swarmed out of the hole in the ground screaming and howling their heads off, and they knocked you down and ran across you, grenade and all, and disappeared into the night like a lot of black bats roused from a cave. If you have, you know what it is to have been really frightened by women. Black.

There's "Spaghetti Farm" coming up. The boys used to call it the Ritz. Had a board up: "Bed and breakfast. Special Terms." Not much left of it now. When the door was kicked open the only thing in the place was a pot of spaghetti cooking. Funny thing, that. Nothing else, except the usual hard board and a bench. No wall-to-wall carpeting for these Italians. Boys ate the spaghetti, straight from the pot. Tried a bit first. Seemed all right. Bet the old girl regretted having had to run and leave her spaghetti behind. But then she could hardly run with a hot pot in her hand. Hardly finished the pot when some Germans gave trouble across the field. So you sandbagged the windows and while the others went off to work their way around the enemy three of you climbed up on the boxes and picked off one German after another as they tried to get away. And you were so busy with what you were doing that you never heard the dozen Jerries come up the cellar steps, silently. You'd no idea they were there. They said there were no cellars in this wet soil. It gave Bert such a turn when he looked round that he fell off his perch onto the floor with a clatter. Just as well the Germans didn't want to fight. It would have been all over. Instead they kept their hands up.

"*Schiesst nicht, Kameraden*" they said.

Jerry either thought there was a whole battalion round the farm or he had "had" his war. Either way, the interview aged you a good deal. Never missed a cellar after that, did you? What the hell is holding up this line? Let's get out of here.

There's what's left of "Charlie's Farm." Charlie copped it there. It's a creepy place. Never felt the same about it since that night. Charlie knew he was going to cop it. He kept talking about it. Gets on your nerves like that, it does.

"Soon be home, Charlie," somebody would say.

"Oh, no," Charlie would reply—almost taken aback by the suggestion, he was.

Bet he didn't know he was going to cop it like that, though. It's a different feeling killing your pals to killing Jerry. Nobody minds you killing Jerry. That's what you're here for. But you have to have a big excuse if you want to knock off your own. There was no excuse here. You were told to stay in the field away from the house—rain or no rain. But hell, it rained so hard you were afloat. So you got into the farm with Harry and another bloke, and you jammed the door. Nobody was going to surprise you. And you sat on the floor of one of the bedrooms with your backs to the wall, and faced the only window looking up to the black sky, and you said what a bloody war this is, and you asked each other how long it would last, and you said it couldn't get worse, and you knew in your heart that was a lie, and you listened to the deluge outside, and you all agreed that it was too dangerous to sleep and you all swore you would stay awake, and you all slept, damn you. And then there was the bark of a gun, and all was commotion and fear, and for one sharp second you thought your heart would burst, and the window was filled with a body and the body was grunting and falling down head over heels upon you. And when you saw it was Charlie coming in search of his fate you thought, "Thank God it's Charlie and not the Jerries, and thank God he got it quick." But Charlie didn't get it quick and he wouldn't die, either, and his life blood sprayed over you and refused to be stanched. And Harry, who had shot him, felt himself part of Charlie's fate and it unnerved Harry, and he shook Charlie and told him he hadn't meant to kill Charlie, and he asked Charlie to forgive him, and he wept, and he asked Christ to let Charlie speak to him. But Christ didn't hear; nor did Charlie, and Charlie died with his blood saturating you as he lay on you, and the blood ran down your legs all warm and sticky, not like water.

"Jesus, that was a near one!"

Merciful Christ, don't take us now! Not now! Why can't Jerry leave you alone until you get off this damned beach-head? Any closer than the last one and you aren't going to make it after all. Why doesn't the column speed up? Herb says somebody's copped it down the line and they're cleaning up. Doesn't matter where you go as long as you get out of this lot. You are so nervous you are prepared to run into the sea aren't you? No future in this. Is it any wonder that the boys here and on the southern front are beginning to beef? Perhaps you're getting tired? Something wrong since Africa. Lord, please take Jerry away just for a few more hours. If you get out now the war might end while you are away. You might get drafted home. Only those comrades who march with you through the night know how much you yearn for home and peace. You don't talk about it. It's a tryst you share. These are your brothers. The others will never know. And those who survive and go back will be misunderstood and eventually despised by the men who stayed home and who don't know. Is that not what happened to your father when in 1915 they carried him home to Blighty gassed at the second battle of Ypres? Later on, he couldn't get a job and you went hungry.

"Follow your conscience, lad," he'd said, "but don't look for gratitude."

Only those who have marched with you will know what you have endured.

Never seen so much wire as there is round here. Place is like a fortress. The light is coming. Doesn't help to see the grave diggers starting so early. Pity the poor B's going the other way. Look at the gun team going up led by a dispatch rider who is either too tense or too starched to sit on his bike properly. Sight of the dead waiting to be buried put him off a bit, didn't it? Soldiers look different when they're stiff. It says in the book that reinforcements shouldn't see the dead, but you can't be choosy on a beachhead. Bet this is the first time this lot's seen action. They've got a lot coming.

There's "Grandpappy's Farm." One of your first farms. There was just Grandpappy and Grandma. Two old, old people. True peasants, independent, individuals. The old folks hadn't run for it with the rest. They couldn't run for it. They could barely walk. There they sat like molting hens on perches, not talking. Livestock had gone. Family had gone. Food had gone. Can't work in the fields. No friends. Can't last long. Refuse evacuation. Refuse food. Grandma clutches a framed picture of their only son, killed in the war. Not this war, the last war. She presses her lips to the glass repeatedly. Grandpappy says he was born in that corner, pointing to a heap of stones by the bed.

"*Nascita*," he says, "birth," pointing with his stick; "e morte, e morte," turning over the dust with the end of his cane.

He was right, he did die, right there in the corner on his perch. His old lady survived him a few hours, then she fell off her perch too. Her eyes had been closed since the old man died, her wings down, feathers drooping. End of road. Merciful she went. They were carried to the cabbage patch and buried together side by side. There's an enormous shell crater where the cabbage patch was. Wonder where the old folks are.

Look at the crisscrossing vapor of the planes in the early morning sky. Sometimes when you lay on your back and looked up they were like a lot of flies buzzing about on the ceiling. You have to watch them or they're down on you in a flash. Treacherous flies, those. Hawks would be a better name for them. Only forty-eight hours ago you watched a truck go up the road laden with stores and troops. You were a few yards from it in the truck behind. One minute it was bouncing along in and out of the shellholes. The next minute it disintegrated before your eyes, limbs, equipment, wheels, engine, turning over and over and landing in the fields. Chaotic. Mesmerizing. You only knew it was a plane when it flashed over the Alban Hills. Treacherous flies. Remember when the visiting generals came sniffing and snooping around the front? And they drew a bombing. And you leapt for your hole. And you looked up and you saw the little white eggs come slithering, sliding down. And you saw the visiting generals like one man dive under a laden truck. And you knew it was full of ammunition and according to the book should not have been there. And it crossed your mind as you ducked and counted the thuds, and felt the earth shake and shudder, what a jelly of generals there's going to be! And when the generals crawled out one of them took a look at what was in the truck. And they went away, palelike.

Remember this road? This is where you came in. Funny you should wait for the boat to get out where the boat brought you in. Going to lie up here all day. Town's too dangerous. Get off tonight. What's this mob by the side of the road clapping their hands for? Well, that's really something. That's the first time in four years in action that you've seen one group of British soldiers clap another group on the battlefield. Didn't think you'd done much, did you? They do. What will soldiers do next? Kiss each other? You should clap for them, poor bastards. They're staying. And they can cop it just as much along the beaches here as where you were. Bit embarrassing, marching past this shower with all this clapping going on. Makes you feel you want to blush. Why don't they turn it in and get back to their digging? Not decent, this clapping. What's this? Thanks mate. That was a good swig of tea the bloke gave you, wasn't it? Right out of his own mug too. He didn't say a word but you saw the bloke's eyes. Stirred it with his heart, he did. Must have meant it. No bullshit. They can't have much tea to throw away. Well, perhaps they're not a shower after all; call 'em a mob. Not much farther to go now. Wonder why those blokes clapped you so much? Perhaps they thought you looked so damned weary. You are.

12

The ship's engines have stopped. Where are we? We are lying in a great heap covering the entire steel floor of an LST. All is quiet. For two months, night and day, come sun, come rain, come cloud, come clear, we have never been free of life-destroying noise. All night the engines have thumped away. Now they are silent too. The silence hurts. Ours has been a nerve-shattering, shaking, tormented world. Silence makes us edgy and uneasy. Water is gently slapping against the side of the ship. Up on deck someone is calling out. A chain bangs against the side of the vessel. The noise echoes through the great metal box. We stir, light a cigarette, tie our boots on again, throw on our equipment. We are ready.

The ship is gently edging into the quayside. The gulls wheel and call overhead. People are waving. Can't know us. Our people are four years away. Good old Vesuvius is still smoking. And there's Capri, its head standing above the mist. Like coming home. Oh, what a bonnie sound. They're playing the pipes, "Come hame, ye laddies, come hame." That was played after Culloden to rally the remnants of the clans. Well, we've come "hame." Perhaps the only "hame" we'll ever know. It's a little port. Can't see much. There's a gentle mist lying over the quayside and the wooded hills beyond. It's as gentle as the mist that fills the glens on a wintry morn. The pity that "Eat-em-up-Joe" is dead. He'd have loved this mist. A stray shell chopped him coming down the line. They've wrapped him up. They're burying him this morning with the rest. Joe only knew fighting and dying. He had his whiskey until the end. Today he'll be buried on the battlefield and a piper will sound the retreat.

Who are these women shaking our hands? Did they come all the way from home to give us a cup of tea? Oh, the tea tastes good. It's four years since we tasted tea like this. We were sitting in the Clyde waiting to go "doon the watter" and a fair lassie came round and said, "Who would be wanting a goodly cup of tea now? That'll be a penny, soldier," she said. "We'll be keeping the pennies for your widows and your children, soldier, if ye dinna come hame agin." Well, the pennies have long since been distributed, and here the tea is free.

We are in the baths at Castellammare. We stand as our mothers made us. Only the identity disks hanging round our necks remind us of war. We are full of lice and everything that we have has been taken from us. We have been told to scrub and keep on scrubbing. How blessed the hot water feels. Now we are sprayed; our hair is cut; we have new clean clothes; we choose them, they are not thrown at us; we feel reborn. We leave the baths and sit at long tables on the quayside; we are given food. British and Italian women wait upon us. Double rations again. We call it "the spoils of war." The benches are hard to our bottoms. It's funny sitting on seats.

We are marching up the road from Castellammare to Sorrento. The promise of spring fills the air. The bees are stirring. Here is a windowbox afire with crocus. Violets stand beside a cottage door. We have come from a land where all was dead. Here all lives. A lassie presses her face to a cottage window, smiles and waves. There are no trenches here, no barbed wire, no mines, no dive-bombers, no gunfire, no mud, no cry and sob of the human body broken and torn. Here the trees stand as trees should, their waxed fat buds ready to burst with the life to come. Orange trees, lemon trees, walnut trees, vineyards. Birds are singing unafraid. Already we carry our bodies well. We march like men. We have begun to cast off our fears. Our joy now is as extreme as our sorrows were only a few hours ago. We march at ease. We are free men. There is no discipline. No orders are given. We carry our weapons and our helmets as we will. Have we not survived?

The pipes are leading the first battalion. Sometimes our ears catch a note thrown back from the mountainside. Someone is playing a mouth organ and we march to the tune—it is a tune our fathers marched to thirty years ago. Here are children playing—children—playing, calling, laughing; unrestrained, frantic, unaware. Snatches of song from a woman by a brook. An old, old man goes by sitting astride a donkey. His cape is wrapped tight around his shoulders. He wears it like a woman, fastened at the back. We call out to him. He smiles and gives us his benediction. A man drives a pig. Hens squawk and scatter. A real live pig, real live hens. A few hours ago we would have pounced upon them and carried them away. We pass a little cubicle house with a bowl-shaped dome.

The road continues upward above the Tyrrhenian Sea. The bright sun of midmorning has dispersed the mist. Down there, almost at our feet, lies the island of Capri in a cobalt sea.

"Capri, Capri," we call. We try to say it as the native says it, not as a name but as a loving promise. One night, two months ago, as the sun began to sink between the upraised arms of land that is Capri, we had sworn to return. We had pleaded with fate that we might see Capri again. Well, there it was as lovely as ever, beckoning, waiting, lying in the sun, telling us we were safe, alive, and that we had returned. Here is our first piece of blossom. A soldier runs, breaks it off, and puts it in his hat. We have halted before a school.

We were billeted on the floor of a large schoolroom. It was the most beautiful room in the world. It was still. It was safe. It bore a roof, which at night robbed us of the moon and the stars but sheltered us from the rains. It had walls, which protected us from the wind. It echoed only to our movements and our voices. We knew only the room; and outside the room, beyond the headland, there was the sunlit sea, Capri, and the sky. We belonged to no one. We were left alone.

Our flags were furled. Our drums, stilled. Fate had cast us out of the cauldron of war. Fate would cast us back again.

We wrote letters, ate, drank, slept, washed, and gambled. We walked along the coast throwing stones into the sea. We echoed the gulls' cries, climbed the hills, threw ourselves down on Mother Earth, and rested. The earth was warm. It surged with the promise of new life. It had not been despoiled by war. In this corner of Italy the plowshare was supreme.

Twice a week the liberty trucks went to Naples. The vehicles were crowded. They lurched drunkenly down the narrow coastal road. We were covered in dust. Most soldiers wandered the streets aimlessly. There was nothing to buy. Nothing to do. Then they went home to a little pile of blankets and equipment on a schoolroom floor. The "wild ones" made a beeline for the brothels and the demon wine. They came home later with a military escort and broken heads. It wasn't possible to stop fighting suddenly. All of us were overtense. We drank with a grim determination to get drunk. Then, we fought. There was blood and glass everywhere. In a drunken stupor we slept where we fell.

We are restless. We go in search of women. We know the risks. Doc said that we were sticking our pricks where he wouldn't put the heel of his dirty boot. Doc is worried. He says more soldiers fall from V.D. than from bullets. But as one old-timer said: "Which would you rather have, laddie, a dose of V.D. or a packet of shrapnel up your arse?"

Padre says it is sinful to lust after woman. Last week, we were expected to kill man.

We are young. We have lived with death. We fear death. We grasp at life. We are outside a brothel in Naples trying to find courage to go in. Some very nice girls are coming out. We are encouraged. We go in and see what is on. In our hands we carry our hats and our money. The questions we ask of the girls cause embarrassment. They are confused. They eye us shyly. We have made a mistake. Mother superior appears. She is German. She is very old. She does not scold us. Slowly, she leads us to the street. She takes our hands and presses them against the pure white starched garment on which hangs the cross.

"My children," she says in Italian, "in the name of Christ Jesus our Savior go home."

We wish we could.

Good brothels are expensive and we are going straight. Besides we are almost broke. But the Italians have great warmth, and spring is coming. We are on the Via Benvenuto. We have a large bag of oranges. There is just time to catch the last liberty truck home. We drop our oranges. They scatter in all directions. A mother and daughter help us to pick them up. Great smiles. Giggles. Uncontrolled laughter. We drop our oranges again.

"Poverini," says the elder of the two women with great tenderness.

Dawn. Four backs against a whitewashed wall. Pips and

peel everywhere. The hurried ride back along the coastal road, bouncing about on the margarine and the bacon. We left behind us in Naples every penny we had. Yet no penny could ever pay for the enormous compassion for a common fate shown us by two Italian women. In their bones they had charity; we know only the fear of death.

Captain Cyril O. Prattfall of the Army Education Corps was lecturing on the four giant evils of war, sickness, unemployment, and ignorance. When he introduced discussion of his last great evil—ignorance—one fat soldier fell off his chair in fits of laughter.

The incident didn't lessen Prattfall's enthusiasm. He wiped his bespectacled, molelike face, balanced himself on his little feet, and returned to the attack. "Ignorance," he insisted, "is the root of all our troubles." He turned the word "ignorance" over and over in his mouth, savoring it, tasting it, as a bon vivant might taste good food or wine. As he held his spectacles before his mouth, his little tongue darted out repeatedly to clean the lenses. According to him, the war was merely a skirmish for what lay ahead in Britain when peace came. With victory against Nazism and fascism, the real struggle against sickness, unemployment, and ignorance would begin. He urged us to prepare ourselves to fight these giants, especially the giant evil of ignorance.

"Ignorance, ignorance, ignorance," he intoned as he continued his ablutions. It was obvious to all who listened that Captain Prattfall had fought the giant evil of ignorance all his life and would fight it to the end. "Ignorance," he held, "has caused the war, as it has caused all catastrophes; ignorance will perpetuate it."

Without ceasing the flow of words, he then fixed his audience with an accusing stare until some of the soldiers shuffled uncomfortably. "Where is Russia?" he demanded. Far from being able to tell him where our chief European ally was, most of us had only the vaguest idea where our chief European enemy was. A North of England lad had told him that "Germany is up't boot." Presumably it was to be found at the top of the leg of Italy. Another soldier had said that the Germans were to be found lying on the French. While the troops roared with laughter, fear must have gripped Captain Prattfall's heart.

What lay completely outside Captain Prattfall's grasp was not the ability to talk. He had done nothing but talk all his life. Never had a word defeated him. He could talk without notes, without pause, without breathing, without rest, without food, without drink, without meaning, without scruples, without end. What eluded him was the ability to think. Like a squirrel in winter he had stored up in his mind an immense supply of nuts of knowledge. At least a squirrel had the sense to eat the nuts and digest them. But not Captain Prattfall. Knowledge to him was not something out of which wisdom might grow. Knowledge was something you amassed in your head to be fired in salvo after salvo the moment the giant evil of ignorance showed itself. There was no thrust and parry, no compromise, no doubt, no reassessment, only an unending barrage of words until ignorance was dead or had fled the field.

Yet the men to whom he spoke were deaf to all his words. Of war and sickness we had seen too much, especially the sickness that war had brought to the innocent people of this land. Of ignorance? We knew our inadequacies. That is why most of us remained silent. In any event, was the matter to be put right by this torrent of words or by these little tracts on current affairs which Captain Prattfall distributed to the troops with the fervor of an early Christian missionary? As he walked across the compound he would carry a bundle of these tracts in front of him as Xavier had carried the cross.

"The problem of production," Captain Prattfall argued, "has been solved. It remains for us to work out a proper system of distribution. Do you men realize that the proper application of scientific principles in a modern economy, as well as the application of scientific principles to the whole process of life. . . ."

The voice went on and on, out through the windows, across the fields, across the bay, and into the sky.

Just look at the bee on the window. It has work to do, must let it out. The bushes outside are beginning to burst their buds. Look at the way the sea ripples away down there. Imagine, such tiny ships to take troops and reinforcements to the front. Wonder if that's where we are going? Don't like the speed by which we are being made up to strength. A number of "little Jesuses" have joined us from England. Hope for their sake we don't go back to Anzio. Maybe we'll go to Cassino again. Not much to choose there. Who knows, we could be lucky. There must be somebody wanting good clean soldiers in Britain. Oh, hell. What's the good of worrying. Bad news from home, though. Got to worry about that. Wonder if they're going to survive the war any more than us? This afternoon we must be off over the hills again, lie in the bracken and sleep. Forget it all. Nobody can touch you when you're asleep on top of a hill. And when you waken you can watch the clouds. They're not worried about the war. There'll always be clouds. They drift so easily. They let the whole thing carry them along. God, how many times have we slept in the heather? Clouds are clouds, whether you see them over Scotland or over Italy. They make a damn better job of things than we do. Must get back to Capri again. Wonder what Jerry was up to over Naples last night? Damn well nearly came through the schoolhouse window as he screamed down the bay trying to dodge the flak. What a wonderful feeling being able to turn over and say to yourself: go to sleep, laddie, he's not after you. Jesus, Prattfall's still talking! If going home means occupying Prattfall's heaven on earth where everybody is going to be sweetly reasonable with everybody else, then most of us would prefer to stay here. He's weird, is Prattfall. The sap must have run out of him when he was young and it's never returned. How complicated and barren can a human being be. Knows about everything, does Prattfall, except flesh and blood.

Prattfall's gone. Couldn't take it anymore. The soldiers were plain mean. Bumped into him, broke his spectacles, yawned at him, snored at him, threw his papers through the windows, and eventually gave him fleas. Soldiers and fleas combined, that's what's done it. Wherever Prattfall slept the fleas went into bed first. He was drenched with them. They were put in every garment he had. A collection of fleas was made daily, some soldiers giving generously, so that the supply might not give out. Those fleas loved Prattfall. They wore him down. They leveled him. He was always grabbing at his knee or his ribs or his bottom. Kind of upsetting for a civilized man like Prattfall. But they did it—he's gone. Don't know where. Some say he jumped into the bay.

Now we are left with our four giants of evil, and it serves us damn right.

"Private Herbert Cudderslip 2345809 reporting," roared the sergeant major marching me in.

Well, there's a cheek, I thought. I'd been wandering southern Italy for five days like a Buddhist monk with my blanket, my tin mug, and my spoon, wondering what the hell was happening to me, and there's this cove saying I'm "reporting." The only thing I had to report was that five days ago Battalion had told me to report to Brigade. Brigade didn't know what to do with me. They told me to report to Division. Division didn't know what to do with me. They told me to report to Corps. Corps didn't know what to do with me. They told me to report to Army. Army didn't know what to do with me. They told me to report to Army Group. Army Group didn't know what to do with me. But they had to find out fast or I'd have jumped the old boat to Merry England. So there I was standing in front of my first general in four years.

"Are you the Private Cudderslip," the general said, "who started his military career at Chelmsford in England four years ago?"

"That's me," I said.

The General beamed: "Cudderslip, can you remember having written a letter to a British radio manufacturing company suggesting a modification to one of their field transmitters?"

Well, I was flabbergasted. It all came back in a flash. Four years ago I'd written to a radio company putting them straight on a simple matter. It was my civvy job so I knew what I was talking about. I'd never got a reply. The sets continued to come out with the same little fault. We always modified them ourselves before taking them with us into battle. After a year or two I realized that this was the way all wars are fought, daftlike. Well, for this I'd won myself an interview with a general in a palace.

"Let's see, Cudderslip," the general said to me, beginning to turn the leaves of an immense file. "You wrote the letter from Chelmsford early in 1940."

"That's right," I said.

"Then you went to Croydon."

"Sir."

"Then to Inveraray, Scotland."

"Sir."

"Then to Greenock for sailing."

"Sir."

"Ah," said the general, turning more pages, "we almost got you at Greenock but off you go to Egypt."

"Sir."

"You disappeared en route," said the general looking up.

"That's right. Put in at Cape Town. Ship holed."

"Then when we wrote to Cairo you were in Tobruk. Then when we wrote to Tobruk you were in Cairo. Then when we wrote to Cairo you'd gone. Cudderslip, where did you go?"

"Greece and Crete," I said.

"So that's it. Should have known that's where you were, Cudderslip. By the time we heard you were in Cyprus, you were back in Cairo. We thought we had you in Cairo but you gave us the slip and we chased you right across North Africa, in and out of hospital, through Pantelleria, Sicily, and the foot of Italy. Cudderslip," said the general, closing the file, "my staff has been chasing you for four years. We had to send you to a beachhead where the Germans wouldn't yield and you couldn't get off to make sure we got you. If you'd have broken through to Rome . . . !"

The possibilities of what might have happened had we broken through to Rome and beyond kept the old cove quiet for a minute or two.

"Cudderslip," said the general eventually in a friendly tone. "Four years ago I was instructed to charge you under military law, I quote the War Office letter: 'For ignoring the appropriate channel of command and for using uncensored mail to discuss military equipment in a manner not conducive to military discipline.' Ever since I got that letter," the general went on, "the file *re Cudderslip* has haunted my correspondence with the W.O. I had come to the conclusion that *re Cudderslip* was going to haunt me for the rest of my life. As it is I'm going to return this file to the W.O. and mark it 'Cudderslip caught.' Some little fellow in the W.O. is going to go home to his wife in such a pleasant mood that his wife won't know him." With that the general shook my hand. "You'll never know, Cudderslip," he said, "how glad I am you didn't manage to get killed. As it is, *re Cudderslip* is dead. Go back to your unit, soldier. If an officer were allowed to drink with a private I'd buy you a drink. Good luck, Cudderslip."

"Well, thank you, sir," I said and saluted. Just as I was going through the door I decided to ask him about the modification I'd put forward to the radio company four years ago. So I turned round and said, "Excuse me general, what did happen to my letter?"

"Good God, Cudderslip," said the general, looking hot, "this file doesn't deal with your modification. This file simply says 'Catch this silly bastard and kick him hard for talking out of turn.' Go, Cudderslip! Go!"

We're going back to the beachhead. We've known it a few days. Feel miserable. Any old where but there. The brigadier thought we should have a concert on our last night. We converted the schoolroom and tried to make a go of it. Bit melodramatic. Didn't come off. We do things by extremes. Dinner was all right. Roasted spuds. Enormous ribs. Cook wouldn't say whose ribs, but they tasted all right. Lots of booze. Somebody even took the trouble to put up colored streamers. We didn't have any balloons. So we dyed a lot of contraceptive sheaths and blew them up. We sparked up for a while. Especially when Smudge and Lofty fell off the stage dressed up as a horse. Wonder is they didn't break a limb. Perhaps they meant to. Darkie and Bert tried to be acrobats. But Darkie had lost his touch. Instead of catching Bert he missed him altogether and Bert sailed through the air and fell on the brigadier. Eric sang "Danny Boy" and made us all feel worse. He'd have sung "South of the Border" if we hadn't stopped him. Damn lot of enthusiasm we would have had for singing "for tomorrow never came" when we knew that tomorrow we'd go back into the line. Cyril, wearing a wig, took off a tart with two brassieres over his battledress filled with spuds. Cyril is a dispatch rider. Bit of a daredevil. Has the Military Medal. When other dispatch riders turn back they send Cyril. He always gets there. He picked up a box of brassieres from a shop when we first bombed Cassino. Only thing he could find. He wore one over his tunic as a joke. Now he always wears one over his battledress in action. Sort of a lucky charm. First time we'd seen the brassieres while resting. He got fourteen curtains. Good type, Cyril, anything for a laugh. So the night went on. It finished with Captain Hamilton striking a serious note on the piano. Old "Hami" leaned over the keys, intent, listening, as if he couldn't believe that the notes coming out were true. He went off in a world all of his own searching for something that he badly needed. The fellows sat quiet, not understanding, as on a church parade. The officers came in with more bottles of booze. They filled our tin mugs for the last time and we drank a toast to the regiment, "God bless it." Then, we all stood again and sang "God Save the King." I've never seen so many fellows fall over during the singing of the national anthem.

So ended our little party. But what kind of a party can you have without women? The booze was best. Helped us to forget.

Morning. We are outside the schoolroom on the road. We are on parade. The regiment is now back to full strength. The rain is coming down in sheets. The hills and the sea are lost to view. Can't wait for the rain. We are wearing our helmets. Under our groundsheets, which are our only cover (and our only beds), our weapons are reversed to keep out the wet. The colonel has just gone to the head of the column.

The orders ring out: "Battalion will march in columns of threes. Battalion, right turn. Quick march. March at ease."

A thousand men respond to the commands as if they were going home. Instead, once more we have entered the web of war. We're off. There's time for a quick glance back at the most beautiful room in the world. It is lost from sight.

We are going down the mountainside. It is still pouring with rain. The rain runs down the soldier's helmet in front of you, down his glistening cape, which covers his back, off his cape down his now soaked legs, off his legs into his boots, out of his boots onto the road, off the road by a thousand crevices and cracks into the gutter, from the gutter it races downhill to the sea. All is being carried downhill, drawn irresistibly to the sea, uncontrolled, like us to our fate. Some

men whistle. Most are silent. The drums and pipes are covered. We approach the port of Castellammare. The ship is
waiting, steam up. We are wet and cold when we embark.
There is no hot tea this time. The quay is deserted. It is best
so.

It is dawn. We are lying off the beachhead waiting to go in.
The port is under heavy shellfire. These are siege guns.
Now and again a building close to the port is struck. The
air-raid alarm has been given and our vessel is turning
around quickly, making for the open sea. All the vessels are
on the move. Why the sudden panic to get away? Where are
the airplanes? There is only a solitary plane flying high
above the Alban Hills. It has fire belching from its tail.

A piece of fuselage breaks off the burning plane and falls
twisting and turning in the direction of the port. What is
this strange thing falling upon us? Every ship and all shore-
based anti-aircraft batteries are now firing at the object. The
sky blackens with shell bursts. But why do we fire at a piece
of burning fuselage?

The object has now swung around as if controlled by a
hidden hand. It is making for the largest warship. The ship
makes a wide sweep chasing its tail. Its guns are blazing. Un-
cannily, the object pursues it, banking, drifting, twisting,
turning. The movements of the vessel cause a mountainous
wash. The object strikes the warship's afterdeck. There is a
monumental, volcanic explosion, ear-splitting, terrifying,
entrancing, infinite. An enormous cloud rises in the morning sky. A gale sweeps the harbor. Debris falls over a wide

area. Where a great warship had been there is now a bubbling, gurgling, disturbed, oil-covered mass.

"Hell," says a soldier, "this is no bloody start to make."

On shore the shelling has stopped. Our troopship swings round hurriedly and makes for the quayside.

13

A soldier in full battle order wearing his steel helmet sat at a little table in a dugout, struggling to stay awake. On the table were two hand grenades, an English newspaper, a small carbide light, and a field telephone. Around him were his comrades, lying in heaps, fast asleep. Some had buried their hips in the cold earth; others lay on wooden doors dragged in from neighboring farms. Several of them lay on their backs, snoring, a dirty rag thrown over their heads. Two soldiers had wriggled under the table to avoid the falling dust. Weapons were at hand. Empty cardboard field-ration containers were scattered on the ground. A ghostlike voice came from a pack radio asking other voices to "report." The draft caused the lamp to flicker and spit as it cast its shadows against the damp earthen walls.

The phone buzzed. The soldier started from his half

sleep. The time was one A.M. C Company was worried about noises. There was a great clanging going on out there in front of them. What's happening? Were they tanks? Had B Company reported anything? Would he ring back? The soldier made his way over the sleeping bodies to the entrance of the dugout. Wearily, he climbed the steps. There was no moon, only a few stars. It took a little while for his eyes to accustom themselves to the dark. Then he saw the outline of one of the sentries, standing against the side of the trench. For a minute or two the soldiers stood on the trench side and peered through the wire. Except for the exchange of fire between batteries in the rear areas, and the sound of the night fighters in the sky, all was quiet. The burial parties had returned, the wounded had been evacuated. Out there, where the battle had been fought, the cap of night had fallen upon a burning, tormented earth.

The soldier went back and called B Company.

"C Company has the jumps," he said, "talking about tanks on their doorstep. How is it with you?"

"Quiet. Why does C Company have to get the jumps just now? Haven't we been through enough without that crowd giving us the creeps at night? This is the first time in days and nights that we have been free from incessant shelling and bombing and C Company has to get the jumps. It's always C Company. Sometimes we have to fight Jerry and C Company. We'll put over some flares."

"O.K. C Company tried flares, saw nothing."

"Look. If we're happy here we'll call C Company ourselves and tell them to turn it in or go and have a look for themselves. Ten to one the clanging comes from a harmless

Jerry mending his boots! If we're not happy we'll soon be back. O.K.?"

"O.K. 'Night. What's left of it."

" 'Night."

B Company rang off.

The soldier buzzed Battalion. Yes. Battalion had heard. A small patrol had been ordered out. Until they reported, there wasn't anything anybody could do except watch and wait. The day's reinforcements and supplies were already on their way up the line. Brigade knew what was going on. They said the whole front was quiet. Supply areas had been hit, the port had just been bombed, but that was somebody else's war. The soldier buzzed C Company again. But C Company still wasn't happy.

The soldier eventually replaced the phone. It was one-thirty A.M. One and a half hours to go. But his eyes would not stay open. For a moment or two sleep claimed him. Gently he slid out of the war, only to be dragged back again with a start by the periodic buzzing from Battalion.

"Able reporting. Of course, I'm awake. All is well."

The soldier allowed his gaze to fall on his sleeping comrades. They trusted him as he trusted the sentries outside. This was the only security a soldier had. He belonged to this group of men. He must not let them down. These men who nestled their heads against his great muddy boots under the table were part of him now. To him they were mother and father, brother, and sister, especially mother. He needed to cling to them as they needed to cling to him. He mustn't fall asleep.

He turned over the newspaper, but the lines of print kept

slipping. Anyway, the news was stale, and it told of a world that the soldier hardly knew. Looking at the items of news he wondered if he had ever been there. It didn't include this bunch of soldiers lying here in the mud, plastered with dirt from head to foot, with sweat and tear marks lining their muddied faces. Nothing in the newspaper about their floundering about in the dark in fields of bottomless mud or running along ice-covered ditches with bullets and grenade splinters passing through their clothing and putting the fear of hell in them; of their being pelted by rain and hail and sleet until their bodies were saturated and frozen; about the lice they carried; or their suffering from trench foot. He only had to look at himself: the hands before him holding the newspaper were broken and cracked, the nails torn and gray. Look at his own battle dress, ragged and caked with mud. His companions looked bad enough, but what did his own face look like? The other day he'd looked in a steel pocket mirror, and what he'd seen had frightened him. It showed an old man with a deeply etched face and a stubbly chin whose eyes reflected intense strain. How could it be him? He was only twenty-three. His age said he was twenty-three. But his body wanted nothing but peace, like old folks wanted. It wasn't possible that these haggard-faced men lying around in the mud were the same fresh-complexioned young boys who had disembarked with him four years ago at Suez to fight in the Western Desert. These men in the dugout were old men. They weren't the boys he had known, full of fun and mischief.

He looked at Pete lying in the corner with his body doubled up and his head drawn down covered by his arms. Four years ago Pete was bursting with fun. Remember when, on arrival in Egypt, he and Pete had bought a packet of filthy pictures from an odious-looking Arab who had stood outside their railway carriage window. The filthy pictures had proved to be six identical pictures of Blackpool Tower! And they'd all roared with laughter at the slyness of the Arab and their own stupidity. They'd laughed so hard that they'd nearly fallen out of the train. He and Pete and the others didn't laugh like that anymore. It wasn't always easy to tell these days whether a man was laughing or crying.

He concluded that the bunch of boys he'd known bursting with life had never existed. He'd dreamed it. They certainly weren't the same men lying on the earth around him now. These men lying in the mud were a species apart. They didn't belong to that other world. They'd always lived in the mud and the filth with their wits scared out of them and that's how they'd end up. It was their lot.

The soldier looked at the newspaper again and then cast it from him. His life was here.

The buzzing phone jolted him from his dreams. It was Battalion. No, nothing. How is C Company? Still no news. Ah, well, the night was passing.

For some minutes he watched the blanket covering the entrance to the dugout as it puffed itself out and then fell limp when the breeze had passed. It never kept the same shape. In it he saw all kinds of figures. The puffed-out figure reminded him of Uncle Henry. In that other world he'd lived in—the world before the war in northern England— Uncle Henry had played an important part. He'd brought him up. On a bitter night like this the family would have sat round a roaring fire. There would be talk of the village, and work and school. And then before they turned in for the night Aunt Hetty would serve a hot drink and hot scones dripping with butter. Then the fire would be banked up. The teapot and cups would be set out for whoever got up in the night. It didn't matter whether you wanted tea in the night or not, you nearly always got it. It was put at your bedside without a word being said. If you slept through the night you could wake up on a winter's morning with three cups of tea, all stone cold.

The phone buzzed again. Yes, he was still awake. It was C Company. They'd lost contact with their forward positions. No, the clanging had stopped. All was quiet. They'd sent somebody out. Yes, they'd call B Company and Battalion.

The soldier checked out his own positions on the buzzer. All was quiet. All safe. In an effort to stay awake he lit a cigarette. No good thinking about Uncle Henry and Aunt Hetty. Only makes matters worse. Home was too far away. Survival was all that mattered. Nothing else made sense if you didn't survive. The only thing he knew was to fall asleep at night and ask, "Shall I see the dawn?" And when day came to ask, "Shall I see the night?" No good trying to reason out this mess. There just wasn't any reason to it. They weren't in charge of the war anymore. The war was in charge of them. Survival and sleep. That's all that mattered now. In the early days when some of the fellows had been blasted out of this life into the next, he and his pals had asked Padre where the dead men had gone to.

"Gone to?" Padre had said, disbelievingly.

Then, he'd quoted I Corinthians 2:9 to them: "That eye

hath not seen, nor ear heard, neither hath it entered into the heart of man, what things God hath prepared for them that love him."

Well, they couldn't get past that. Padre had one over them there. All they had to do was believe. They hadn't bothered Padre since. These days in Italy they never talked about where you went to when you died, they only talked about not going. Survive! That's what you had to do. But you needed an awful lot of luck to do that. No matter how bad things got, you wanted to survive. What was the good of talking of fighting for freedom if you were cold stone dead?

The phone buzzed. It was B Company. They'd lost touch with their forward positions. C Company were in the same boat. No replies were coming in on the emergency radio link. Better look out! The soldier started out of his dreaming. He buzzed Battalion. The line was dead. Grabbing the radio handset he called Battalion on the air.

"Hello Roger, Able reporting."

"Hello Able," came back the reply, "Roger here."

At that moment a great wailing and howling blotted out all conversation. He quickly switched to the alternative emergency frequency. There was just time to hear Battalion calling out the code name for general alarm when that too was blotted out by a great caterwauling.

The soldier was wide awake now. Fear had suddenly gripped him. He took a whistle from his pocket and blew it as hard as he could. He ran out up the steps into the trench and blew it again. He continued to sound the alarm as his sleeping comrades awoke and staggered out of the dugout, adjusting their steel helmets and clutching their weapons, cursing. Running back into the now empty dugout he tested the buzzer once more. All lines were dead. He grabbed his two grenades and his rifle and made for the door. Others were sounding the alarm down the trench. As he ran up the steps a rocket arched its way across the sky. Suddenly it exploded above the British positions, casting a great red glow across the earth. For a moment or two the flare stood there in the sky unmoving, shimmering and twinkling and bathing the defense works and forward positions in a deep red light. Then, hesitatingly, reluctantly, the flare began its gentle descent earthward. As it did so, the whole sky across the entire front was lit by the flashes of the German artillery. An enormous barrage had begun.

Allied Force headquarters, Caserta Palace. The general sat alone at a rough, blanket-covered table. He rubbed his eyes with the palms of his hands and took up his pen. For a moment his attention wandered from the sheet of paper before him to the movement of men and vehicles passing through the grounds.

The general's thoughts were occupied with the outcome of the battles being waged on the Anzio beachhead a hundred miles to the north. Perhaps the time had come to issue some special order of the day in an attempt to rally the Allied forces to still greater effort. He had just returned from a visit to the front and he had not liked what he saw. There was, in fact, precious little of the beachhead left. He had never witnessed such incessant bombing from the Luftwaffe anywhere else in the Mediterranean theater. There could be no question of successful evacuation. If the last defense line was pierced or, as the more pessimistic-minded staff officers thought was probable, the Germans leapt behind them with the use of airborne troops, slaughter or surrender would result. Defeat at Anzio would cast a gloom over the whole Allied effort and would probably result in the Russians being more difficult than ever. Anzio must be held.

No good holding postmortems at this point. There would be enough of those when the war was over. The fact was that the Germans had reacted sooner and with much larger forces than they had imagined possible. And once the Allies had lost the initiative, they had never regained it. Of course, the Germans had been helped by a lack of drive from the Allied side. But all that was in the past. Not a tittle of that could be undone. What to do now? That was the question. In his long military life it always had been the question.

In landing at Anzio they'd taken the long chance and it hadn't come off. Well, that was the fortunes of war. War was "Hey diddle, diddle, the cat and the fiddle," except it was events, not the dish, that ran off with the spoon. Now they were stuck, the whole hundred and fifty thousand of them, in a little box of wet, freezing earth, roughly four miles wide and five miles deep. They couldn't go forward— Intelligence now showed them to be facing overwhelming odds—and they couldn't go back. Indeed, at all costs they must not go back. This wasn't another Gallipoli or Dunkirk. There weren't the ships, for one thing. Well, they'd have to stay there. So much depended on them staying there. But could they stay there, in those numbers, on that little plot of ground, dominated as they were by the enemy guns, within minutes of enemy airdromes and with an endless succession of enemy attacks taking place? The general looked at the little cloth model on his desk. Only the future knew the answer. In the meantime he had to do all in his power to avoid a military disaster. The troops were seasoned and were not the panicking type, but once a rout began in that confined space it would be impossible to stop it. If any words of his would help the troops he'd better write them now. Soldiers and ships were in very short supply in this theater, words were plentiful.

The general took his pen and wrote down the leading words of his Order of the Day: "With our backs to the sea . . ."

A gray dawn. Leaden skies. We have fallen back and are lying out in a field. The enemy is separated from us by a water-filled ravine. Jerry is in a hurry. He's been bringing up reinforcements in half-track vehicles. He unloaded them right in front of us just out of small-arms fire. They came rushing across the field, shouting, as if they were racing each other to the beach for a dip. Crumpled green-gray all over the place. We are dug in in twos and threes in small craters; some of the craters are already half filled with water. We've been told that until reserves come up we have to hold this line. We must not go back. Is it true that in some parts of the front Jerry has overrun the forward positions and is behind the gun lines? That puts him a long way past us. We are being held in front by fire while Jerry works in from the flanks. Jerry must have infiltrated our main defenses. In our little sector alone we've seen fourteen tanks go by, some of them Tigers. If he gets into the Padiglione woods we'll never get him out. There's scattered fighting taking place behind us. You can't mistake the sound of a German machine pistol. We cannot stay here—too exposed. Once he gets our measure he'll flatten us. One minute we are firing for all we are worth, the next we are told to get out. Again, retreat is the order.

But where to? If we run across the field we'll be knocked over like ninepins. The road? The road is a chaos of vehicles and corpses. There is only one place to go, Carroceto railway station. Down the ditches we go, doubled up, lugging the ammunition boxes with us. Drag the mortar. Work our way around. Lot of smoke. Don't bump into Jerry. That would be stupid. The road is under heavy fire but we've got to get across. Don't stand there. Run as if your life depends upon it; it does. Has Jerry overrun the strong point in the station? It's under fire from the other side. Come in, cautiouslike. No, we're all right, our pals are here.

Merciful Father, listen to the bombing. Never had so many German planes on our heads before. Well, at least the R.A.F. and the Yanks are up there hitting back. But the bombs are falling too close for comfort. Here's a good old British tank coming along the causeway. He'll sort Jerry out. Big fellow, him. But he's got his problems too. Jerry's got a self-propelled gun firing at him. Tank doesn't like the gun. With his gun muzzle flashing and smoking the tank is trying to get himself round the back of a big haystack. But he's slipping and sliding all over the place in the mud. *Wham!* Jerry fires short. *Wham!* Now too long. *Wham!* A bull's eye. Poor sods. The tank and the haystack are burning together. With the tank in the station yard we could have made quite a show of it.

Hey, you! Stop thinking of yourself. Do what you're told and go back and help bring in the wounded and whatever ammunition you can lay your hands on. Of course, the whole place is smoke and falling dirt and screaming splinters. What do you expect? Move fast, Jerry's all over the place.

Heaven's name, the fellows coming through the smoke along the ditch are not ours, they're theirs. They're shouting and firing. Drop the wounded and run for it. Easy now. Sorry mate. Good luck mate. Through the smoke, up the line, and into the station. Now don't stand there telling us how close you were to being killed. Dig as fast as you can. Faster than you can. This is the first time you've dug a defense position facing the sea. That means we're surrounded. We can't run away if we wanted to. The last man in from Brigade says that a strong counterattack is under way. They should break through. Here there are sixty of us with ten wounded. That's a grand number, and we have a whole railway station to ourselves, including a great locomotive. The locomotive stands in front of the ticket office (*Biglietteria* it says) with part of the station roof on its head. Looks sort of sheepish. Wonder where the engineer went to with his greasy rag? The Italians knew what they were doing when they built this place. It's been well and truly bashed about but it still is one of the strongest places on the plain. Come on, fill the sacks. Get dug in. Only two things you can do now: fight or surrender. No talk of surrender. Anyway, what have you got to worry about? Jerry isn't bothering us now.

The party coming down the railway line has broken off the engagement. We've got the wounded into the blockhouse. We've plenty of weapons and the station is swimming in water. Food and ammunition have been shared out. Could hold out for a month here. Especially with our two antitank guns. The lieutenant doesn't have to tell us this is a big show. Just listen to it. Like the great waves of an angry sea rolling along the entire front. And look at the smoke.

It's midmorning. The battle has gone beyond us now and we're stuck out here on our own. We've no connection with the rest of our division except for a weak radio link. Lieutenant knows what he's doing. He's kept his head. Without him our initial terror at being overrun might have got the better of us. He's got his posts out. We are buried in the middle of a pile of rubble that used to be the station W.C. Our view is up the railway where it swings round a corner. First German who came round we just knocked off. We pressed a button and he went *plop*, right in his tracks. Like he was in a dream. If his rifle had been a fishing rod you'd say he was skipping school and going fishing for the day. Fellows behind him were craftier. They tried to snipe us out so we put some mortar shells over and that's the last we heard of them. The fishing fellow just lies on the track, all on his own, with one of his legs stuck in the air.

Now Jerry has become very cheeky. It's midafternoon and he's obviously decided he wants us to move out before dark. He's been pounding the station with mortar fire from the north while he put a company-strong attack in from the south. The rest of the station roof has gone, including an observation post we had up there and the blokes with it. Fellows at the side of the station being attacked said that Jerry was overconfident. On he came, in broad daylight. Machine gunner said he didn't like to kill them quite like that. Of course, they were repulsed. We've lost ten dead and we've two more wounded. Jerry's dead are lying all over the bottom track. There's a great heap of them under a little bridge that crosses the railroad.

It's dark now. The lieutenant has drawn in his posts around the blockhouse. Just as the sun was setting Jerry brought a self-propelled gun down the track and blew us out of the pile of rubble. We are well entrenched now farther back. Except for the blockhouse every wall is down. The mortars have been falling since late afternoon. Even before darkness came we were so covered with dust that we couldn't recognize each other. You can only see the fires that are burning at different points in the station through a curtain of dust. The self-propelled gun made an awful mess round here. Great beams of wood were splintered all over the place. It was touch and go with that fellow until we'd got his measure. First time in four years we've been fired at by a heavy gun at point-blank range. Quite frightening it was. The shell has such a velocity at that range that you think it's going to slice the world in half. We don't know if we killed the self-propelled gun or not. Got dark, thank the Lord. But at least he isn't firing. Jerry has been using some shells with delayed fuses, which have turned the station into a hellhole. You don't know which part of the station is going up next. We are having difficulty finding room for the wounded now. They can't all get into the blockhouse. Blockhouse is for fighting, not for dying. They say Jerry has pushed our lads right back. But Brigade told us to hang on. Help is on the way. The air force has pounded and strafed Jerry all day long. The navy fired in from the sea some of the biggest shells they have in the box. They must destroy an area the size of a football field. Pity if our own blokes kill us, but it looks as if they might. Can't blame 'em if they clobber us with the rest. We're no more than a pinhead on the map. There's a real battle going on now. It's eerie to hear the tanks go clanging by in the dark and wonder if they are going to turn into the station and knock you off. We are open to attack from three sides. Until now we've held the little bridge over the track but we can't hold it much longer. The lieutenant is not using flares. His order is, hit back if you're fired at; otherwise we are guarding our ammunition. He says we are going to have a bad night. Somebody managed to brew up some thick hot tea, which put new life into us. It is bitterly cold. A drizzle of rain has set in.

The lieutenant was right. It's midnight. A scrap broke out just south of the station. Instead of our comrades coming to our help we had to go to theirs. You couldn't stand by and listen to your own fellows being killed. We managed to get a number of them inside the station. Jerry tried to catch us off balance while we were trying to get the new fellows in. He made a determined attempt to rush the blockhouse. The one thing we really feared was a flamethrower. We have no stomach for that. Shrapnel's bad enough, flame is worse. It smells so. Fires are burning in the station. That's twice Jerry has tried to rush us. There are thirty of us now, including the reinforcements. Where to put the wounded has become critical.

It will be dawn soon. All night our hopes have risen and fallen, flickered and died. Jerry has given us no letup. But there's a lot of fight left here. We used one of the antitank guns to clear Jerry out of the end of the station, but it seemed to have no effect on the pile of rubble. As soon as our gun stopped firing, the chattering of the German machine gun began again. You couldn't budge. So up Sarge got with his automatic gun over his arm and was off. He didn't ask for volunteers. If he'd have asked for them he wouldn't have gotten any. Nobody wanted to follow him out there. But we just couldn't let him go off on a goose chase like that all on his own. Sarge is not that bad a bloke. We cleared the station with bayonets and rifle butts. Somehow Sarge has survived but others have gone. We didn't want prisoners. But we've got two, whether we like it or not. How can you kill a man when he's clinging to your boot and beseeching you not to kill him? We've put them with the wounded in the blockhouse.

Our radio link has died. Before first light Jerry sent down the line a creepy, crawly, tanklike thing the size of a sofa. We wondered at first what on earth was coming. Gave us the creeps. We fired our machine gun in the direction of the noise, but whatever it was, it kept coming on, slowly. What on earth was it? Couldn't be a tank. It wasn't heavy enough. There wasn't the scream of metal tracks. But we couldn't see. So we got one of the antitank guns into position and fired a flare. There it was, a sinister object coming for us in spite of all our fire down the railway track. The antitank gun hit it first shot. There was an enormous flash. If there was a man inside, the explosion must have caused him to vaporize.

We all gave a great cheer. But almost as we cheered, there was a second flash and the antitank gun and those around it were torn to pieces.

We have repulsed the attack that followed. Of the two tanks that entered the station yard one is smoking, as good as dead. The other was holed but managed to crawl away, dragging itself across the dark rubble like a great metal crab with one of our blokes clinging to it trying to get a grenade down the turret. But we've lost both antitank guns now and there are only twenty of us left. Unless help comes soon we're finished. It only needs one determined tank or self-propelled gun crew to do the job. Only time our spirits rose was when one of our brave little artillery spotters hovered above us in a gray, overcast sky and then cleared off.

The two German prisoners seem grateful for the chance to nurse the wounded. Some of us even feel warm toward the Germans as something we have saved out of a dark night. Germans and British are all mixed up now. Some of these wounded will surely die if they are not gotten out of here quickly. The Germans say that a great offensive has begun to throw us back into the sea. We are too exhausted and desperate to discuss it. There isn't a single man here whose face isn't ghostlike and whose hands do not tremble. Do you expect us to discuss who's winning the war? One of the two German soldiers is covered in blood from head to foot. Blood is nothing new, but we've never seen a man dyed blood red before. Even the tunic belt with the buckle GOTT MIT UNS is dyed red. The blood has paled, but it's blood all right. He told us that while they were sheltering under a bridge an enormous shell had fallen and the comrade standing next to him had simply exploded and drenched him with blood. One moment he was talking to his comrade. The next moment he was scraping him off his battle dress.

Another gray morning. The front is on fire and German machine guns are chattering nearby. Heavy mortars have driven all of us into the blockhouse. Most of our fellows are lying out there in the rubble now, dead. Some have their lifeless faces turned to the sky; some are without faces. Either way, they couldn't go home now, not without a face. It's as well they're dead. We dragged one wounded fellow into the blockhouse under the little ghostly light. It was too late. We bundled him out again. Poor devil he was. He didn't only have to put up with the war. He was a ghoul on top of it. There's always one. His pockets were crammed with little things he'd taken from the other corpses. Crammed. Must have risked his neck a dozen times. Some years ago a fellow like this would have turned your stomach, made your flesh creep. We don't feel like that now. He's just a curiosity. We don't resent him. He's dead, isn't he? He didn't create all the corpses. We did. Why is it always the little fellows who are the ghouls?

Some of us would rather be outside than in here. The noise of the machine guns firing through the walls and out of the sandbagged windows is deafening. The cry of the wounded crammed and cooped up in this little place is hard to bear. For their sake some of us would surrender now if we knew how. The place stinks of antiseptic and cordite and bodies. Mercifully for us, the cloud of dust and the green, yellow sickly smoke protects us from the bloodshot, questioning, burning eyes of the wounded. All we can do is stick a fag in their mouths and light it, and, when we have time, hold their hands, or place our hands on their foreheads. Some of the wounded struggle so hard to tell us so much. But what is there to tell? Of what use are words now? We do our best to calm them. But they clutch at our clothing, cling to us and draw our ear to them. Others, more hurt, either lie silent, resigned, wrapped in their bloodstained greatcoats, peaceful, or breathe deeply, laboriously—unconscious of all around them. Much of them has left us.

We shall make our last stand here. Whoever rushes this place will pay dearly. Yet, we're scared of a gun; we're scared of a flamethrower; we are probably scared to die. And after all we've been through. We can't last long. How long will the war last? At least we've seen another dawn. We only ask to see another night. That's not much, is it? Those of us who are close in comradeship have exchanged messages: ". . . if you survive and go home." It is in times like these that those with children seem to have special strength. They will go on, they say. Something of them will not die. But most of us in the blockhouse haven't had time to have children. When we die everything of us dies. We are fruitless.

Gone quiet. The Germans have ceased to fire on us. They're busy firing somewhere else. The lieutenant is looking out. He seems excited. What is this? Merciful Lord, this cannot be! It is. There's a battle going on at the southern edge of the station. See those tanks? They're British. Those infantrymen are British infantry. Among them are some of the "Micks." Did we not tease each other during the night and call, "Send for the Micks," the fighting Irish! Well, what is left of them is here. Won't push these boys back easily. They love a fight. They are coming for us. Oh no, we shall wake up and find ourselves still trapped in this cage waiting for death or imprisonment. But it's not so. They are British troops, and they're outside, and there are lots of them. Those of us who can still fight burst out and join them. They've opened up a corridor to the main front. We can get out. All is not lost. What did Jerry think he was doing, talking about pushing us into the sea. We'll push him in. That we will. Thank Christ for another chance, or as Padre always said after events like this: "Laus tibi, Christe."

A staff officer at Caserta Palace was studying a great wall map of the Anzio operation. He stirred his tea slowly as he continued to study the map.

"You've got this all wrong. Good job the old man didn't catch you. We lost Carroceto during the night. I've been up most of the night watching it go."

A hand reached out and removed a flag that marked the position of a British infantry battalion. It was laid aside. After much discussion a German flag was advanced in its position, slightly. The discarded flag inadvertently fell into some tea slops and was later tossed out.

14

Lieutenant Pritchard Russell tried to make himself comfortable against the cold barn wall. Men were sitting about, eating and drinking, smoking, talking quietly, lying in heaps snoring, or just rubbing their bloodshot eyes and thanking the Lord they'd survived. Explosions in the vicinity caused a cloud of fine dust to fall from the rafters upon them. The lieutenant listened for a moment and then turned to his writing.

"My dearest wife," he wrote,

my source of strength and hope and happiness. Thank God I am able to write now.

John will have told you of the lucky chance that brought us together before they took him back to you. I was helping in the evacuation of my own wounded when my eye happened to fall upon the identity card of one of the other soldiers lying on a stretcher on the quayside. It was John! We'd been fighting a life and death struggle on the same plot of ground without either of us knowing the other was there. Can you imagine the reunion—especially as I have not seen any of you for four years and John has recently seen you and our son. John was weak from his wounds; I was overjoyed at seeing him and hearing at first hand of you and our child. A quayside full of the dead and the dying is the right place to cry. I'd say he and I had only two or three minutes together. Two or three minutes after four years! But what is time? Give John my love. I hope they have put him in a hospital where you can reach him. The few minutes we spent together were perhaps my saving. I have seen so much senseless slaughter these past three weeks that I had begun to lose heart.

I don't know how to say it but Andrew has gone. He was a few yards from me when he was struck by a mortar shell. All I could do was to get down on my knees and hold him. He lasted a minute or two in my arms with his head on my shoulder and then he gave a quiet sob and was gone. I took off his ring, as I'd promised I would, and God willing, I will bring it home to Nellie. She is going to need you now. After Andrew's death, I found myself walking across a field regardless of cover. I am sure you were there to protect me or I would have been killed.

I am now out of the line, safe and sound, with several days' beard on my face. I cannot remember when we came out. I cannot honestly say if I have been here one night or two. It is all so hazy. Now it is daylight and we have rested and the world seems better. "Tubby," the whole 225 lbs. of him, has just trundled in with a great mug of steaming tea. I'm sure we both say "Thank God for Tubby." He and I have been through so much together.

His greeting, *"Fine old sort of a morning, sir,"* has never changed as he has handed me my first mug of tea. You could hug Tubby sometimes for being so placid. Hami's batman was just in to tell us that during the night a great hulking shell went slam-bang underneath the dugout where he and Tubby were sleeping. It was a dud, or so we hope. Hami's batman said old *"Tub"* was the first to roll out of his blankets this morning. *"Cor 'Arry, come and see what's sticking up in our backyard,"* he called. I felt like saying to him, *"Bit of all right luck you had last night, Tubby? Not often a siege gun fires under your bed."* But I know what he'd have said as he handed over the tea: *"Funny old war this, sir,"* so I said nothing.

Here I am writing about John and Tubby when all I want to say is how much I begrudge our separation. If we were to tell anybody that we have had only four weeks together out of four years of married life, it would sound so ridiculous. And yet it is true. And the most beautiful thing about all this hardship and trial is that instead of my love for you growing cold and dying it burns always with an ever brighter flame. In my darkest moments, I can always feel your presence and your strength. Even after Andrew's death when I became confused at the utter insanity of it all, there was still that spark of you in me telling my spirit not to surrender. We really don't ask anything of life except just to know the unbounded joy of meeting again. Was it yesterday that I climbed your college wall and caused a rumpus by coming crashing down through the glass of the watermelon frame? No, of course not, yesterday was the day I came and threw pebbles at your window and we climbed the college tower together and watched the dawn come on the first day of May. We wanted so little, we asked for so little, we needed so little of life except each other. And then the war came and I came to tell *you I was leaving and my eyes betrayed me before I had spoken and you clung to me and we wept, and you were with our child, and I went away across the seas; and in going away we were not farther apart but closer together in a way that no words can tell. All this we have known, and knowing it we shall never be alone in the world again. Pray that out of this crucible there will come a better world for us all. Sacrifice on this scale cannot be in vain.*

Do give all my love to our son. It is strange to have a child running about and talking and yet never to have seen him. The picture I have always kept close to me is the one you took of him crawling through the orchard with the apples he had picked up stuffed inside his shirt. His face glows, and his eyes sparkle with mischief and fun and innocence. To know that the trees back home still bear fruit gives me faith. Nature knows no pause. The blossom will come again and the bees will hurry in and out of our garden, the robins will nest in the hedgerow and greet the dawn. How wonderful, beloved, if with this there is joined our own laughter and the call of our children.

The issue here must be settled soon. If we knew why we started the war we have long since forgotten. Most of us just want to go home—alive.

Goodbye, my love, my dearest, own, own love. May God keep you and our son always. That is my dearest wish. We have lived so little together yet we have known the fullness of life. Be glad of heart.

> *Ever and always,*
> *Your loving husband,*
> *Jock*

Lieutenant Russell took up another piece of paper and started a letter to Nellie. But somehow the words wouldn't come. He had known Andrew and Nellie too well. And the blow of Andrew's death was too recent. He had found himself staring at the paper and thinking of all the little things he remembered about Andrew. He'd try again later on. These letters of condolence were the very hell to write; each one was an ordeal and a torture. He knew that an incalculable human life, unfulfilled, had been snuffed out like a candle. Not just a life in terms of a number, but someone who had been part of his life for years; someone who had marched with him, sung with him, shared his hopes and his fears, prayed with him that the African sun would go down that they might breathe and that the Italian sun would rise again that they might have warmth; yearned with him for peace and to return home. Perhaps someone who might have been spared had he himself not erred in leading him. There was nothing left now except a memory and a little pathetic bundle of personal belongings, which had been recovered from the corpses and which now lay at his feet.

After a while, the lieutenant gave up the letter writing and turned to deal with his lice.

Mrs. Ronald Allenby opened the letter from Lieutenant Russell. She was not moved by its message, but only by its kindness. The War Office had already told her of the death of her Ron. She was still living in a daydream. Nothing mattered anymore. Nothing came. Nothing went. Nothing moved. She read nothing, heard nothing, saw nothing, ate nothing. Life had come to an end. But here was a young man who had fought with her Ron and was still in the greatest

danger taking time to write this sweet letter. She was moved
to reply. She ought at least to say thank you, and to wish the
young man well. So she took pen and paper and wrote:

Dear Lt. Russell,

*I would like to say thank you for the kind letter of sympathy you
sent me on the death of my husband, Ronald Allenby. I had already had the sad news from the War Office so your letter came
as no surprise. Nor did it reopen any wound. The wound is not
closed. He must have had a premonition he was going. His last
letter ended "Do not grieve if I cannot stay."*

*I am glad that my husband got on well with you all. He's
often mentioned you in his letters home. I read what you said
about his having died a hero's death. But I didn't want my husband to die a hero's death. I wanted him to come home to me.
That's all. I don't think he and I would have known what a hero
was. We wanted to do what was right and proper. But we did so
pray for the day when we would be together again. That's all we
wanted. We only had each other. We didn't really know much
about the war. Now I am alone in the world. There's no family
on either side and no children.*

*You ask if there is anything you can do for me. Well, if you
could have anything that is left of my husband's personal belongings sent to me I should be most grateful. I appreciate your
promise to see that his grave is cared for and that a proper cross
is to be erected.*

God keep you and let you return to your own loved ones.

> *Sincerely and gratefully yours,*
> *Ethel Allenby*

It was some weeks later when Ethel Allenby was feeding her
cat in the kitchen that she heard the click of the letter box on

the front door. Going through she was puzzled to see the letter she had written to Lt. Russell lying there on the mat. But it had a great stamp across it which said: "Returned to Sender. Addressee Killed in Action. Refer Next of Kin War Office Records."

"Oh, dear," she said peering at the letter in her hand and feeling very bewildered, "Lieutenant Russell has gone, too."

Then she placed the letter under her late husband's portrait on the sideboard and went back to feeding her cat.

15

Private Thomas Woodcocke slid down to the bottom of the shell hole again and lay still. He was terrified, panic-stricken; as a fighting man he was finished.

All around him the earth was in convulsion. Clouds of smoke and great cascades of earth darkened the setting sun. Periodically, showers of dirt and stones rained down upon him. He had no idea what had happened to the others. The whole of his body and his senses were pulverized, bruised, numb. His head was splitting with pain. He was running with sweat, yet he was freezing cold. He had vomited all over himself. He had had enough. This must be the end of the world. He knew it was the end of him. No one could emerge from this artillery barrage alive.

Private Woodcocke's war had been a short war. This was his first time in action. Only three weeks ago he was on his honeymoon in Devon. He'd always remember the little inn at the mouth of the rivers Tor and Torridge: the red earth, the salmon, the great seas that came in, and the spray flung against the casement windows at night. Well, that was three long weeks ago. Here he was about to die.

You've got beginner's luck, Sarge had said as they had set out that afternoon. Beginner's luck! To get to Anzio when the fighting was at its worst!

The whole thing had been a nightmare from beginning to end. Their departure had been delayed hour after hour throughout the day. Eventually they had jumped off an hour ago, in company strength. Their objective lay a couple of football fields' distance away. It had all looked so simple on the map. Only this sector of the line was quiet. Extraordinarily quiet, they said. There might not be anybody there. That's one of the things they had to find out. They were to run in, test the front, grab what prisoners they could, do the reconnaissance expected of them, and run out again before Jerry mounted a counterattack. If they could go in on light ground and hold the position until reinforcements joined them, so much the better.

And what had actually happened? Well, they'd got out in no-man's-land all right, and then, smoke or no smoke, there had come crashing down upon them the fury of hell. The intensity of the barrage and its accuracy had shaken the old sweats. At first Private Woodcocke had run like a startled pheasant. Then he'd stuck to four other soldiers and done what they'd done. But they'd all gone. When they got up to run they'd toppled over like lead soldiers. The last one had struggled up the side of a ravine with him, only to throw up his hands on getting to the top and fall backward head over heels into the deep water that lay at the bottom. Now he was alone, on another planet. For all he knew about what was going on or where he should go, or what he should do, he might as well be on another planet; at least there wouldn't be this vicious howling, screeching, lashing shrapnel ready to tear him apart.

Yet he couldn't lie there trembling from head to foot waiting to be killed. He'd be lost if darkness came, and the longer he stayed out here the more likely it was he would be killed. If the Germans followed their barrage with troops he'd be trapped. He knew that if he ran in the direction of the setting sun while it was still light he would come to his own trenches and his own people. They were not far away. Once darkness came he would be doomed. Yet he couldn't get back through this shellfire. He'd already stuck his head out of the hole and tried it. He must wait a little longer.

As he waited he watched a great fat brown sleeky-looking rat that had suddenly entered the crater. It was running round and round the sides of the crater squealing and squawking as if it were in pain. It never stopped. Round and round it went, skidding and slipping and crying. It reminded Private Woodcocke of the motorcyclists who had ridden the "wall of death" at the Easter fair back home. This was a wall of death all right. What was the rat looking for? Had it lost its young in the barrage? What a filthy rubbery tail it dragged after it. It was the size of the rat that astonished him. He'd never seen a rat that big in England. It was almost as big as a cat. He didn't know rats existed that size. At first he had been afraid of it and had lunged at it with his bayonet.

It took not the slightest notice of him. It ran across his legs repeatedly.

Suddenly the barrage shifted in the direction of the British line. Now's the time to run for it, thought Private Woodcocke. Better a shell hole closer to home than out here. He scrambled up the steep side of the crater. He looked over. He looked directly into the face of a German soldier who was crawling forward on his elbows. The meeting came as a shock to both men. It was such a shock to Private Woodcocke that he lost his hold on the lip of the crater and fell backward clutching his rifle. As he fell, the German's face appeared over the crater's edge. It was the first German soldier the Englishman had ever seen. He had a rifle. He looked as terrified as the Englishman felt.

Private Woodcocke lay at the bottom of the hole watching the German who was crouched at the top of the crater. He was a big fellow, covered in dirt.

Why doesn't he shoot me or run me through? Private Woodcocke thought. Why don't I shoot him? The safety catch is off. All I have to do is swing the rifle up, point it, pull the trigger. If the German tries to jump on me I'll stick him with my bayonet.

But, try as he might, the Englishman couldn't move a muscle. He was fixed, rigid, paralyzed.

Why not cry out for mercy? he thought. Why not laugh, smile, show him you wish him no harm? Offer him a fag. You've no argument with him. You need each other. Tell him to go off into another hole. Tell him you won't shoot him in the back. You can't. Tell him you'll go to another hole.

There was only silence between the two soldiers. The German stared at the Englishman. Each transfixed the other.

Suddenly, the German began to shift his grip on his rifle.

That's what he is going to do, Private Woodcocke thought. He's going to club me to death. Now he understood why the German had not already shot him or knifed him. The end of the German rifle was twisted and broken.

One moment the German had been edging down the side of the crater on his bottom, with his eyes fixed steadily on the Englishman's face, the next moment he had leapt to his feet and had brought the butt of his broken rifle down heavily on Woodcocke's head. Dazed from the blow, and fighting to retain consciousness, he brought his rifle across his body in one mighty sweep. There would be no second chance. The German grabbed the rifle and a tug-of-war broke out between them. The Englishman lay on his back and grimly hung on to his weapon. If he let go or fainted, all was lost. Meanwhile, the German pulled and pulled.

It wasn't a German pulling at all. Woodcocke was in a small fishing boat off the Devon coast fighting with a strike so heavy that his first reaction had been to cut the line. Instead he hung on, fought it, whatever it was, played it as it twisted and turned, heaved and pulled. Eventually, he brought his quarry to the side of his little boat and looked down into the saddest dolphin's eyes imaginable. Horrified, he cut the line with one blow.

Slowly, Private Woodcocke regained consciousness. His rifle lay across his knees. His hands remained frozen to it.

He was dimly aware of a figure standing before him. It was
the German, legs astride, resting on his upturned broken
rifle, swaying gently as if a little drunk. He was silent. He
was looking down at the Englishman. Private Woodcocke
raised his head and looked into the German's face. Instinctively, he turned away. The man above him had only half a
face. Where his chin and his tongue should have been there
was a great welling bloody mass. The blood poured and
spurted out alternatively as if someone were opening and
shutting a tap. The lower part of the face, including his chin
and lower teeth, were hanging down in front of him on a
thread. The dying man's eyes were close to his. They looked
at him with unspeakable sadness. Suddenly, the German
pitched forward and came to rest across the Englishman's
knees. Private Woodcocke fainted again.

The Englishman awoke to a star-filled sky. There was
sporadic firing. Abruptly, the whole nightmarish horror of
his ordeal returned to him. In the dark, he felt for the dead
German. He could not find him. He felt his own legs. They
were wet. He felt his bayonet. There could be no mistake.
But where is the dead man? he said to himself, as he made a
wider sweep with his hand. Perhaps he had imagined the
whole thing? Perhaps the wet on his trousers was his own
vomit? There is no German, he said aloud. There never was
any German. As he spoke, one of his hands fastened on a
hard round object. He took the object in both hands. An
intense nausea overwhelmed him. In his hands were the
German's teeth and part of his lower jaw. He was repelled.
His immediate reaction was to cast the object from him as

far as he could. Instead, for a moment or two, he sat with it, holding it. Then he rushed out of the crater into the dark night, screaming.

*

A big, ungainly man sat in a ditch,
Dressed in dirt-stained clothes.
Wiping the sweat from underneath his helmet.
Smiling, friendly.
Watched by a wide-eyed Italian child,
Who looks upon the Negro's face, disbelievingly.
"Fall in! March!"

A broad back, ambling down the lane,
Hung pedlarwise.
Black fingers reaching out to caress
The strings of a guitar
Held by an astonished refugee.
Yassur! Yassur!

16

A pockmarked, smoke-covered land, dotted with burning vehicles and abandoned equipment. A helmet in the mud with a hole in it, a map case, a torn coat, an airplane sitting in the treetops, bizarre, forlorn. Broken bodies: a hand in a puddle, a foot sticking out of a trench, a scarecrow of a man hanging lifeless from the black stump of a tree, an airman lying alone in the middle of a field wrapped in the silken shroud with which, hopefully, he had parachuted to earth. Neat rows of corpses with lifeless faces, burial parties, wordless. A soldier searching for his comrade: "Have you seen Larry?" A soldier in a wood, bending down, with the black smoldering stumps of trees around him, scraping together what is left of his comrade, putting it into a sack for decent burial. A long line of ragged wounded (ours and theirs) hobbling back, ambulances that never stop, a man painting large red crosses on hospital tents already riddled with shrapnel, a blonde nurse lying on her side among her patients, dead, with a little red cross upon her white blouse, loaded hospital ships swinging away out to sea. A wounded Englishman leading a sightless German boy across a field, alone. Great tank-recovery vehicles lumbering down a shell-pitted road with their cargoes of broken steel and broken flesh. More distraught Italians (God knows from where) struggling to the port. Men searching among rubble. The splashes caused by a man throwing pebbles into a pond. A tiny glassed-in shrine of the Virgin standing intact at the entrance to a destroyed village. Young men with old faces lying out at the front, waiting for the assault to be renewed and talking in cracked voices about Tom and Dick and Harry who once were and now are dead. The tense faces of the rearguard, holding the escape gap open. "Are you the last, mate?" they say. A small group of glum-faced senior staff officers, deep beneath the ground, staring at a map, silent, wondering what the hell to do next. A gray sky that has looked down on the worst and the best deeds of man.

Men arriving at the port. Fresh men, scarce men, new men, marching up the road with a confident tread; fed men, slept men, clean men. Heavy guns, barrels still cold, racing to the front, eager to claim their share. Brand-new tanks rolling onto the docks. Aircraft in the sky looking for a fight and finding none. Supplies, oceans of equipment, mountains of arms coming ashore, looking for humans who will use them. But weary men seek not equipment; they seek to sleep and to forget.

The smell of the dead, sweet and sickly, of men rotting, of

bloated dead horses and cattle, of smoke, of sweat and dirt, of louse powder, methylated spirits, and soap. The overwhelming, revolting stench of a pile of dead rats lying in a field.

The sound of the wind, blowing in gentle gusts, trying to put out the flames. The odd burst of gunfire from both sides, daring the other to move, gunfire that is no more than an involuntary twitch compared with what has gone before. The sound of men whose voices have changed. Men snoring. The *pop* of exploding lice as the purifying candle flame is quickly run up and down the seams and corners of lousy clothing. The cry of the wounded. The sobbing of a boy soldier sitting in the corner of a barn, alone, weeping. An older soldier sitting with his back to a wall looking at the sea and peacefully talking to himself. The sound of marching feet, dragging feet, trailing feet, the rattle and the roar of vehicles, the faraway voice of the surf, the siren of a ship at sea, the shuffling of a deck of playing cards and the calling of the odds by four soldiers dressed in tatters gambling in the shadow of a well in a farmyard. The sound of a soldier playing a mouth organ sitting on a tomb in the civilian cemetery. The sound of rats gnawing on something in the cavity of a farm wall at night. The hoot of an owl. The tapping of a beetle. The oaths of a man who stumbles over a stone. A bugle sounding the Last Post, its notes thrown back from the hills and the sky, grave and beautiful.

"They say the 5th has gone."

"The 5th? They cannot have gone under. Not the 5th

who fought at Plassey, Waterloo, Ypres, Dunkirk, and El Alamein."

"But they have. The whole shooting match of them."

"But I marched with them. They can't die. Rubbish, man! Listen to the drums and the pipes as they march through the streets of Ayr on their way to Greenock, the Clyde, and the Western Desert. Hark, man, can you not hear them sounding Retreat as they march up and down the beach on the Ayr coast as the winter light fades? See them, as I've seen them: a great shipload of them forging their way in a convoy, southerward, with all those young men clinging to the rigging in the sunlight, and down below, on a hatchway, the pipers and the drummers playing 'Over the Sea to Skye.' Why, man, they'll never die."

"Aye, but they're still gone."

"Look what they did on the road from El Alamein to Tunis. You couldn't kill 'em. They marched, fought, retreated, fought, advanced, fought; they never fell back except to lick their wounds and then go farther forward again. They fought, fought, fought; they never yielded. And when it was all over, cannot you remember how they behaved in the great march past at Tunis? No regiment in the world could have 'ordered arms,' 'sloped arms,' and 'presented arms' as they did. And when they marched past the saluting base in open formation, and the order rang out 'Eyes right!' as the drums tapped and the pipes skirled, why, man, you never saw the blokes on the saluting base (whoever they were); you saw the 5th and all they had done, and all they were, and the sacrifices they had made, the courage they had shown. You saw their pipe banners carried high, and your eyes dampened, and involuntarily you shed a tear, just one tear."

"Aye, but they've still gone."

"They cannot have gone, man. One night if you'll stay here you'll see them come back out of the darkened plain. The drum will be beating a single tap, they'll be a bit gray in the face, and they won't be carrying their heads as proudly as they usually did, but they'll be here all right. They'll come down the ditches, hugging the cover; they'll bring their dead and their wounded with them, but they'll still come. Make no mistake. And they'll build their campfires again, and make merry, and be lighthearted. And when it's all over, they'll go back over the seas again. And they'll stack their drums and furl their flags, and knowing war they will speak only of peace, and tell their children, 'It was nothing.' "

"Halt! Who goes there?" A sentry peers into the night-covered plain.

"Friend," comes back the reply.

"Advance, friend, and be recognized."

There comes only the sound of the wind.

17

An old general going back,
God knows he'd tried,
A German lance broken,
Massacre averted, the line held.
But not victory.
Guns on the Alban Hills
Looking down on men in the mud.
The Thrower thrown.

An old general going back,
To hear them say:
Why didn't you get on the hills?
They'd show him with colored pencils and flags
What he should have done.
But it wasn't like that.

A band of steel, constant crisis, ditches full of corpses,
  first tanks burned to a cinder.

An old general going back, not bitter, sad,
Convinced that he'd been sent on a damn-fool mission,
Ill prepared, frantically launched, too many cooks
  brewing a broth of overwhelming disaster.
Divided counsel, risks uncalculated, advice rejected.
Hellespont, dice in a can.
In the German, not terror roused, panic caused,
But anger, heroism, and resistance.
Bluff called, the long chance lost.

An old general going back,
To strike his flag,
And watch clever men refight his battle
With their slippers on, writing under the warm glow
  of a desk lamp,
Their bottoms warm, roasted by the fire,
Detached, removed, cozy.
They would tell him
And he would weep, for man.

18

We are in our old holes where the Villa Angelina used to stand. There is nothing left now but dust, lying in great drifts, deep as the deepest snow; dust and rubble, and the ghost of the past. Like us the villa is a sacrifice to war.

These strange charcoal stumps and black stalks sticking up out of the earth are all that remains of the villa's orchard and the copse of trees. They are hideous things, burned, crooked, none of them reaching higher than a man. Look at them in the half moonlight. Are they our comrades who have passed on, coming back? The earth around and between the stumps has been distorted grotesquely. The whole area is littered with stones and rubble and rusty wire, and the flotsam and jetsam of war. Right across the ruins of the house, running between the black witchlike sticks of trees, is a major defensive position. Where the imposing front entrance used to be, empty corned-beef tins, tied to a wire, are clanking away in the breeze.

Is it years or weeks since a great villa stood here? Do you remember? It shamed you at first. The wall mirrors at the foot of the great staircase looked at you accusingly and said you were a mercenary army bent on destruction. Yet you sat at the great polished tables and wolfed your army rations off delicate crockery, and stared at each other's mud-covered bodies and were shy. That was in the beginning when you expected to hurry away to Rome. But the Germans refused to give you Rome, and then you did not have the strength to take it; and then you were told not to take it but to sit in the mud here and be shot at. So instead of knowing peace, the Villa Angelina knew only war. It became a little island around which the battle raged continuously, until it was no more.

But then, a soldier has no use for a house. Not when it's standing upright. Dangerous like that, incongruous. He's better off when it has collapsed, better still in the earth. Houses are for people; here man is a mole. And those soldiers who never knew the Villa Angelina as it was cannot feel sad or glad from what has happened. Shall we continue to destroy until there remain only God and nature?

How long will the war last?

The hush of false dawn. The noise of the atmospherics on the radio lessens. Watching heads nod. Life is suspended; it is neither night nor day. Momentarily, the guns are still. The last dispatch rider to be sent out before the dawn is putt-puttering down the lane. The sound of the German night fighters lessens in the sky. A raven caws. The patrols are in, soaked, sitting, chewing, black-faced, not speaking, eyes staring over their tins of food at the ground, changed, giving involuntary shivers, wondering about what might have been and who was dead.

Men in slit trenches and dugouts half filled with water, half asleep, half awake. Stiff with cold, under greatcoats and blankets. A cold gloomy day, mist, cloud, rain. The pretense at sleep continues. The fleas are awake, pricking and stinging.

"Stand to!"

Hurried movements, curses. The dawn approaches. Some men on rising cross themselves for the day. Most men curse their luck. Standing unfed, unwashed, largely unslept, scratching, belching, peering. Shapes, land, hills, sky appear out of the mist. A meek sun casts its first faint light in the heavens. Stars twinkle and fade. Who has gone in the night? Several. Where are the two "young Jesuses" who came up the line last night? Over there, dead. Their boots sticking out of the bank in which they had burrowed. It's too late to tell them that in the night banks collapse under shellfire and snuff out the life of the uninitiated. What do two lives matter, anyway? They weren't known. Their loss was a number. Leave them where they are. No trench foot for them. Fish them out later on. At one time we'd feel sorry for them. We've gone from feeling sorry to being irritated; now we're afraid of them. They're dangerous.

"Stand down."

Go, sort out your cold, lone cell in the earth. Get your

mess tins and eating irons. Scrounge tea and food. Make sure they hand out the rations of the dead. Dead men's food comes up the line for forty-eight hours. Take it to earth, like a dog gnawing a bone in a corner. Not safe on top. Death sometimes calls his own reveille at dawn. Try to scrounge more tea.

"Is it right, mate, that we're going in tonight?"

What will it be this time: a ridge, a knoll, a heap of rubble that once was a farmhouse, a crossroads, a creek, a water-filled ravine, a railroad bed? Does it matter? It will be bitter fighting without decision, whatever it is. When soldiers rest they rust.

A coldhearted day. The promise of the sun has given way to stormy rain. All becomes sodden wet. But soon the sun triumphs, the gloom lessens, the mist is dispersed, the heavens are more clear. And here a snowdrop full of hope and cheer and delight, telling of a time when all nature will glisten and be as green and gay. And here a long finger of ivy moving on, timeless, unperturbed by winter or summer, war or peace. The mists driven from the plain lie mournful on the Alban Hills. Across the mountain passes a curtain of rain. But there has been another dawn. Shall there be another dusk? How long will the war last? We set out to break the Germans' courage and have finished by breaking our own. Looking down upon us, the hills mock us and have little pity.

A day of hardship, of fear, of tension is closing. A page of life's precious book is torn out and thrown away. With hurried feet the sun makes its way across the land and drops into the sea. Darkness falls. Patrols are preparing to go out, to plod across the country in the absolute dark and return with their nerves shaken. The wind sighs in the wire. A flurry of rifle fire. The chirp of a cricket. The stars reappear. A sharp dispute has broken out between the guns, and the earth trembles. Men are moving off with coils of wire. Others will dig new machine-gun posts. Some prisoners are already being brought in. At the front men wait to be buried. A man with a drawn, hungry face, full of melancholy, carrying a special rifle, is making his way out through the wire, alone. He has the look of a wolf. Well covered against the cold, he stalks the enemy in the dark, and the day. When he will re-turn, whom he kills, how he kills, when he kills, where he gets to, nobody knows. He says little. Men are his prey. The moon lies low in the midnight sky watching him.

Curtains of tracer across the land. Flaming red balls of anti-aircraft fire crisscrossing the heavens. In the dugouts and foxholes only voices break the night. Above ground, men crouch and talk of time a world away, of things known, of things yet unrevealed. Gradually, the circle of faces fades from sight. Then the soldiers nestle together, thinking of a happier past, or suffer dreams with tears and tortures and touches of joy. Here sits a dead German, his back against the trench side. We shake him and he lives and bursts into laughter. We back away, aghast. He dies again. And again we shake him. This time he rises and pursues us with wild laughter. We waken in the cold earth, our faces and our bodies covered with sweat. A great full moon shines down on the Alban Hills, bringing them oppressively near. We lie down in a shiver.

We have seen another dusk. Shall we see another dawn? We are young, shut in, manacled to a plot of ground, sometimes without hope, but never without hunger and thirst, and fear and anger and lust.

How long will the war last?

Days gave way to weeks. Young men grew old. The futility of war hammered at our senses. Was nothing saved? Out of dust and ashes, debris, desolation and death there remained only the nobility of self-sacrifice, the better legacy of death, the only death in which those who looked on could find consolation.

A message cannot be got through. But it must be got through. There is a shuffling of feet, men look away. "Allow me to take it," says a shy creature who until now has lived among us almost unrecognized. A figure astride a motorcycle is swallowed up in the night.

A group of men pinned down at the side of a road. A shell lands in a neighboring gun pit. A direct hit. There are cries for help. To move is to invite destruction. Officers and men hug the road. A soldier gets up and begins to run to the help of others. He never gets there. Lesser men, with their trembling bodies pressed against the road, watch him topple and fall and lie still.

Someone says a wounded Italian child is lying in a gun-swept field, bleeding. Without a word or a moment's hesitation a soldier goes out and returns with the child cradled in his arms.

A German soldier who, when his comrades have gone, stays behind and tears his shirt to pieces to bind our wounds before trying to get away himself.

A wounded man difficult to move who begs his comrades to leave him by the wayside, abandon him, that they might make good their own affairs.

The nobility of self-sacrifice is what remains when the lesser things have fallen through the sieve of life. It is the one thing that answers the aspirations in our own hearts for something more exalted than ourselves; it is the white flame of youth with its appetite for sacrifice. This kind of death is not unredeemed. After four years of war the magic has gone out of most things in life. Nobility remains. It lights the darkest battlefield. If that is extinguished, all is gone. We have become so destructive in word and deed that it only remains now for us to pretend that nobility isn't noble. If we do so we shall draw the blind upon the last hope of man.

19

The seventh corporal work of mercy is to bury the dead. That doesn't just mean your dead, it means anybody's dead. Do it for friend or foe without grumble. It is an obligation that the living owe the dead. There is a pit for all of us if we can find it. If we cannot, others must help. Life has inflicted its hurts, now let the man sleep.

The burial party is standing at the side of the grave leaning on their spades, helmets removed. From the holy book the words are read: "Man born of woman hath but a short time to live. . . ." Sarge throws a spadeful of dirt in on the blanket-covered body; now Harry; now the others. Now all of us, together. The wet earth thumps down on the corpse, providing the face with a mask. Quickly, the mound of earth disappears. A friend has gone. He has drunk his vessel of sadness. His battle is stilled.

Here the dead and the living lie side by side. A soldier can fight in the morning, bury his mate in the afternoon, and fight again at night. To have the cemetery so close shortens the lines of communication. To shorten the lines of communication is the aim of all good tacticians. They couldn't be shorter here unless we fight in the cemetery itself.

We watched the first graves cut. Since then we have been here at all hours day and night. Our calendar has been the little heaps of earth that march away from the sea. As we lurch in and out of the shell holes on our way to the cemetery, the rattle of the engine is accompanied by a tattoo played by the dead men's boots on the floor of the truck.

"Death is the great leveler," says the grave tender.

This man is the only fellow we know who refers to a dead soldier as a "person."

"Please bring this person this way. . . . Put this person down here, please. . . . Let us cover this person's face. . . . Careful, careful, gently," he would say, "this person has been shaken enough. . . . No, no, place this person's head the other way."

Nation, color, rank, creed make no difference.

"A darkie in a white man's grave?"

"Shall we shift him?" we said.

"Oh, no," he replied, looking down on a great black face, which the grave number said was a white face. "This person will rest here just as well as in the next hole. Years hence, it will not matter if white men lament at a black man's grave. The Lord will not distinguish."

"A German?"

"Ah, yes, place this person over here, please. A shallow

grave. We shall lose him later on when his people come for him. They will want him to sleep with his own."

"And this person? You know him not? Never bother. He is known unto God. Gently now. Ah, yes, death is the great leveler. The greatest."

This night we took from a sack the remains of two of our comrades—a father and his only son. We laid them in the earth side by side. Rarely have we dug so clumsily. Never did we treat each other with so little grace. None of us allowed the light of the lantern to fall upon his face.

Wind sighing through the cypress trees. Starlit night above the Tyrrhenian Sea. The clatter and scream of the mobile cranes unloading the ships at the port. Ships on the horizon winking at each other with tired, colored eyes. Glint of the water in the bay. The steady tread of soldiers trudging by. Someone whistling "Colonel Bogey." A voice that penetrates the night and is lost. A strangely quiet front. A war now so silent as to hurt the ears. Swinging lanterns, figures lightly and heavily laden. Little processions coming up the slight rise from the road, staggering in, walking out. Mounds of earth. Quiet voices. "Man born of woman . . ." The thud of falling earth. The click of spades. And so one by one the little cots are filled; the platoons are assembled, "Dressed by the right, all present and correct, sir," resting together as they fought together. May they never tire of resting here above the Tyrrhenian Sea.

"Eternal rest grant to them, oh Lord."

20

The sightless song of a lark high above a battlefield. Gulls, in from the sea. Graceful swallows completing their migration from the depths of Africa and finding their nesting places gone. A patch of blue violets, brushed by the playful wind, sitting at the foot of a black charred stump of a tree. A golden dandelion. A lizard basking on a rock at the bottom of a shell crater. Distant hills drawing upon themselves a mantle of lovelier hue. Gradually, our thoughts succumb to the lure of new life. It is spring. Shall we be home before the leaves fall?

The war cannot last much longer.

Easter morn. The sun rises with new strength, refusing to be waylaid by the clouds and the rain. Some of us wish each other "Happy Easter." Christ is risen. There's a new chance for man. We have had our fill of sorrow. Let us turn our faces to the light. The Italians working on the roads and the docks call out *"Buona Pasqua"* and give us little lambs made of sugar.

Dusk. A commotion on the road: a group of Italians jogging by bearing a flower-strewn bier, on which stands a statuette of the Madonna with a chalklike face. The bearers went by at the double, chanting. There was a fleeting glimpse of animated faces and many bloody knives protruding from the statue. It was quite vital, they told us, that their "Mother of Sorrow" should reach the church of Pietà before dark.

The Abbey of Monte Cassino. A hilltop covered in smoke. The sky filled with bombers, the valleys reverberating to the deep-throated roar of their engines. Siege guns flinging death. The heavy monastery walls beginning to rock. Ceilings falling in. Women and children entombed. Not a living thing left. Oh, poor, pathetic, defenseless Italian women. This is your Calvary. And you are the children of the Renaissance. And we? We are the children of the knife.

Two men in a forward post watching a man carrying a great cross before him down the mountainside—a handful of priests huddled against him. They disappear in smoke.

"They've gone to the old butcher in the Lord's name," says one of the soldiers.

But, no, there they are again, stumbling on. The one in

front holds the cross up high, like on an Easter Sunday morning procession.

The smoke clears. The two soldiers look upon the black burning hulk of what was once a monastery.

"It isn't going to be the same without the old abbey," said one soldier to the other.

"Now everything has the pox. Some people are only happy when everything has the pox."

Cassino fell on the eighteenth of May.

Two soldiers shoveling beans into their mouths nonstop, not talking.

"For Christ's sake," one of them says eventually, putting down his spoon.

"Leave Christ out of it," says the other.

We are sat in our holes watching the Yanks go by. Good boys, these. Troops have been flooding in for weeks. The bridgehead is alive. New gun pits being dug everywhere. Strong patrol action. Miles of wire being laid. Supplies rolling in. Going to be like sardines in a tin soon. Jerry hardly fires a gun now but what somebody or something doesn't cop it. He's making the most of his chances. The sky is red above the port at night.

The Yanks are cocky as usual. Looks as if they don't need

us. Good luck, Yank, if you can end the agony of this bridge-head by yourself. There is inexpressible joy at the thought of breaking the window of our cell and escaping forever from this plain.

They say our fellows in the south are through Cassino and are chasing Jerry up the Liri Valley in the direction of the Alban Hills.

We've been up all night. Knew it would happen. Yanks do it on their own be damned. That would be asking too much. We are going to join them in the general assault. We left our positions at dusk and made our way through broken country of brush-covered ridges and an intricate network of streams and waterways. This is the land we tramped over when it was bare. Now we followed each other through the longest grass. In dead silence we passed through the Kings and turned right up a side valley where we climbed a slight ascent. We halted there for the night and put our posts out. But there was no rest. Instead there were constant comings and goings round our bivouac and whispered challenges and strain. It rained in the night. The party begins at 0545 today, May 23. It will begin with the usual gun barrage. We have been promised a smoke screen and lots of armor. Our job is to secure the Yanks' left flank so that they can get across the Alban Hills and trap the German Tenth Army retreating from Cassino. Our company has to take a farm at the end of the vineyard three hundred yards away.

It's the first dawn. There is the faint outline of hills in the northern sky. Shall we be lucky this time and get on the hills instead of lying at their feet? We are full of hopes again and expectations.

A soldier dragging a heavy object through the mud gives up in despair. "For Christ's sake," he cries at the top of his voice. "Why do we have to be bloodied all over again like this?"

For over a week now we've been fighting in the German Caesar Line. We've run into 75-mm guns housed in solidly emplaced tank turrets. Each strong point is flanked by mobile and fixed antitank guns. In and behind the defenses the Germans are firmly entrenched in the deepest dugouts. The German minefields took a heavy toll of the tanks and the armored tank destroyers. The weather has curtailed the air bombardment. We've had our work cut out to stop Jerry chasing us out of an orchard and down the side of a dike. Campoleone is a fortress. The rising ground is a paradise for defense. Full of twists and turns, ups and downs, dead ends and blind alleys. There was no gully we went along that wasn't blocked. No ridge that wasn't defended. No ditch that wasn't enfiladed by German machine guns. As for the villages and the stone and plaster houses, we laid down a barrage upon them as well as a screening of white phosphorus fire. Then we rushed in, only to be thrown out again. Jerry is in no hurry to leave. Even when his defenses have disappeared behind the dust and smoke clouds created by the bombing, Jerry always seems able to emerge ready to fight again. These boys aren't going to desert their pals fighting their way back from Cassino.

Reluctantly, we draw our forces together for another try. Again we fail, again we have losses. Jerry is a hard nut to crack in defense. No panic, no rout. Retreat, stand, fight, retreat, stand, fight. That takes some doing after four months on the beachhead.

We are red-eyed, hesitant, and trembling. Some of us are detailed to go down into a neighboring wheatfield in an effort to find some of our fellows who are out there moaning. Cautiously, we press our way through the tall crop, searching, feeling in the dark.

It is two A.M. We have done what we can for those we could find in the wheatfield. We are too tense to sleep now, and anyway we are to be committed again at first light. Instead of sleeping we sit in our holes, preparing our weapons, and nod.

"Tell me, Dick. Are we sat outside the Gab Gab gap in the Mejerda Valley hoping to get into Tunis? Or are we sat outside Rome? Does it matter which? Campoleone? Is it January or May? It's May. Dick died in this same vineyard four months ago. God!"

They say the Yanks have failed to get across the Alban Hills and are now making their way across the front of the mountains in our direction. We don't know what to believe. We've run out of morphine.

* * *

We got to the end of the vineyard looking for Jerry and we found a group of Yanks looking for us. They said there weren't any Jerries for miles.

"Look, chum, only an hour ago . . . look, who do you think killed those fellows stacked against the wall? Do you mean to say it's all over? Give us a fag."

Bloke just came in says there's a handful of Yanks in Rome. But Jerry's gone. That means the German Tenth Army has escaped. Who cares? We're still alive.

A piece of warm bread with a piece bitten out of it lying on a trench step tells us how recently Jerry moved off.

A British soldier sits, scraping the mud off his boots; another washes his shirt. Is this what is meant by victory?

Nothing can rob us of the joy of climbing these hills. To look back to the plain and the sea is a rewarding vision. We are climbing the narrow rising lanes to Albano. These are the same lanes that Jerry used. They seem too narrow to permit the flow of an army. The peasants are already filtering back. Squat, solid, teaklike beings, carrying their few possessions on their heads, rounded by tempestuous times, unbroken. Everywhere there are fruit trees, fields full of vine sticks, olive groves, and walled gardens. A cedar with its many layers of shade. A giant oak, its thousands of leaves fluttering a welcome. A red admiral butterfly sunning itself on a stalk sticking out of a white cottage wall. A long row of pines marching down the hill.

Everybody's going to Rome. The conquerors rubbing shoulders with long columns of weary, haggard, blood-stained prisoners. Even a group of drunken soldiers are going there. They sway in and out of the heavy traffic, the worse for having looted somebody's wine, followed at a respectable distance by a little hedgehog on a string. One of the drunks has pitched forward on his face. Now another; still another. Blood on the road. German snipers' bullets spit past us, ricocheting from the stone walls and kicking up the plaster dust. Hell, we don't want to get killed at this stage. The Germans have been surrounded and are being sniped at steadily. Have they got the bastard who killed the drunks? Yes, they dragged him out by the scruff of the neck, unmoved; and before our fellow shot him the German said in perfect English, "God be with you." More shots, but this time only soldiers letting off steam in the sky. That church bell we heard pealing must be the only good one left in Latium.

We move as if in a trance. A perfect day. The sun on our backs, the wind fresh on our faces. Tall grass curtsying to the breeze. A blue sky crowded with planes. We climb upward: one height attained only reveals another. A town all in ruin. A lonely brook. Through crumbling empty streets, past a deserted church, down winding steps cut out of stone, across an aqueduct, past villas with little wrought-iron windows looking onto gardens, under arches. At two in the afternoon we stop to eat by a little tower with a belfry. Some men prefer sleep to food and cast themselves down in the deep grass by the wayside, exhausted. In half an hour we are off again, Bert trudging alongside, and telling us of a dream he had had. He said he had stood at the foot of the Alban Hills looking down on the plain of Latium to the sea. The light was poor. He didn't know whether it was the gloaming or the first dawn. Then he heard a funny scraping noise and looking down the road he saw a little group of men, heads down, hanging together, struggling up the hill. There were four or five of them, some of them hatless, some wearing bloodstained bandages. They were clinging to a tattered rag of a flag. It was only when they came abreast of him and he was about to speak to them that he noticed an officer standing by the roadside looking in a big book, which he held in his hands. The group of soldiers never glanced at Bert or the officer, nor did they look up, but as they hobbled by one of them called out in a low voice:

"First Company, Ninth Panzer-Grenadier Regiment."

"But there are only five of you," said the man with the book. "Where are the others?"

"Sleeping," said the men with the flag as they stumbled on.

Bert said that as his eyes got used to the halflight he became conscious of many other little groups struggling up the hillside. They stretched right down to the sea. As they went by they never looked up. He felt some of them were going to collapse in front of him, but somehow they kept stumbling on, one little group, then another.

"B Company, First Battalion, Irish Guards."

"But there are only three of you. Where are the others?"

"Sleeping." The word spoken like a sigh.

"A Company, First Ranger Battalion."

"But there are only two of you, where are the others?"

"Sleeping."

"D Company, 2/7 Queens Royal."

"But there are only six of you. Where are the others?"

"Sleeping."

They were followed by a tattered figure who showed no face, alone, without a flag.

"Soldier," he said in a low voice.

"Soldier, soldier," echoed the wind.

Then came a group of bedraggled Italians, carrying their infants and their few possessions, silently.

"You know," said Bert, "for no reason at all, when I woke up by the little tower with the belfry I found I'd wept."

Just then we passed an Italian child sitting on the step of a house preoccupied with dressing her doll, a little white bow in her dark hair. We trudged by, ignored.

Is this the road to Rome?

Requiem

We were marching in a straggle along a valley between two of the steepest points on the Alban Hills when we saw him. There he was, over on the right, a German soldier in full battle kit, hanging on to the hillside, head down, kneeling in prayer. "Come over here and look at this," someone called. We were curious, so a number of us went over to look at him. A group of soldiers had already gathered there.

The German boy was dead. Somebody had followed a few yards behind him and, almost from underneath him on the steep hillside, had shot him quite deliberately up through the neck into the head. The telltale powder marks were there. Instead of tears, a trickle of blood had escaped from the dead man's left eye and had made its way across the deep furrows of his dust-covered face. His hands still clutched the wildflowers of the hillside. His slung rifle pointed to the sky.

Seen at closer quarters his uniform was filthy, tattered, and torn. Flies danced on his bloodstained collar.

"That's the best German you'll ever see," said an onlooker, "a dead 'un."

"Christ, he's only a kid, leave him in peace."

"He's lucky, he never knew what hit him."

"How do you make it out any soldier who's seen as much action as this fellow, getting into this fix. Look at him, trying to climb a sheer wall of a hill with his back as a perfect target. Why the hell didn't he get down the valley with his pals?"

"Who's to say his pals ever got down the valley, anyway? This Jerry is obviously the Casabianca type. 'The boy stood on the burning deck.' Noble heart, and all that sort of bull. I'd take a bet that this kid has run and fought all the way from the Garigliano, perhaps all the way from Africa. He left it too late. He didn't want his comrades to think he was going to be the first to quit. He went on firing until it suddenly dawned on him that his mates had gone. He was alone. Then he rushed out and the rest just followed."

"Nah, it was just his bloody luck. Had his number on it. That's all there's to it. It had to be here or somewhere else. Running down the valley, as the first to quit, or scrambling up the hill in panic like a silly goat, makes no odds; he couldn't escape the bullet that had his number on it."

"Don't weep for him. He's only asleep. 'We are such stuff as dreams are made on, and our little life is rounded with a sleep.' By the look of his face it's the first sleep in months. He was worn out before the bullet touched him. His earthly pilgrimage has ended. He will arise. He's praying for us. We're the ones that's left behind. Don't pity him, pity us."

"That's all cock, mate, and you know it. For this kid it's 'finito tutto.' He'll never see Rome again."

"Look, what's one crummy life. Instead of mouthing all this bull, why don't we go through his pockets and whip his kit. He's got a fancy wristwatch there, he has, and a gold wedding ring. Anybody game to take a chance with a booby trap and get this bloke sorted out?"

"What beats me is that somebody deliberately shot the kid from behind. And in the spring."

"What on earth has spring got to do with it? You've got a victory, haven't you? Well, be satisfied. You can't have a victory without a sacrifice. There's always got to be a sacrifice."

The distant wail of bagpipes in the hills. Long columns of men trudging through the valley toward Rome and their destiny.

About the Author

WILLIAM WOODRUFF, born in Lancashire, England, was at Oxford University when World War II interrupted his education for six years. He served with the British Eighth Army's 1st Division in North Africa and the Mediterranean theater, and was in the initial wave of the Anzio assault landings. As a captain in the 24th Guards Brigade, he took part in the battle for its entire duration. After the war, he returned to Oxford and graduated in the arts, took a degree in science from London University, and earned his doctorate of philosophy at Nottingham. The author of many books, Dr. Woodruff is now graduate research professor in economic history at the University of Florida.